Sport & Meditation

The Inner Dimension of Sport

Sport
& Meditation
The Inner Dimension of Sport

Sri Chinmoy

ISBN 978-3-89532-213-6

The Golden Shore Verlagsges.mbH
Austraße 74
90429 Nürnberg • Germany
www.bluebeyondbooks.co.uk

Printed in the Czech Republic.

Contents

EDITORIAL NOTE

Sri Chinmoys words presented here have been selected from his writings, lectures and answers to questions which he offered to athletes and spiritual seekers over the years.

All texts, quotes and aphorisms by Sri Chinmoy unless otherwise noted.
All italicized texts by the editorial staff (except poems and aphorisms).

We would like to thank all the athletes who have kindly contributed to this book by sharing some of the experiences they had during their athletic career:
Bill Pearl, Carl Lewis, François Gay, Katrina Webb, Olivier Bernhard, Paul Tergat, Tatyana Lebedeva, Tegla Loroupe and Ueli Steck.

Foreword
By Olivier Bernhard

For me, sport is meditation. Athletes in many sports speak about experiencing a state of energy flow when being in perfect balance with their mind and body. It is a state where pain and fatigue do not exist. I can still remember, it was at the Duathlon World Championships, I was getting off the bike to put my running shoes on. The first time I realised that I was running, I had already passed the 10km mark. It felt like my feet were not touching the surface of the road at any time. I was sure that I was just dreaming it. I had tears in my eyes. I was not pushing myself nor was I aware of being in a very important race. I felt as if outside of my body and felt that somehow I myself was not performing. Those very special and rare inner moments still mean a lot to me.

All of my life any sport activity has been connected with strong passion. As a child I had the urge to run around and be outside most of the day. Later, as a professional athlete, I realised that besides the physical there is another higher level. Some call it the mental, some call it the heart or soul, or even a dimension beyond that. By becoming conscious of this inner dimension and by training it, I overcame obstacles that I could not have overcome if I had trained the body only.

I soon experienced that true sports is not just pushing your body to new limits. To become a complete athlete you have to train your inner capacities with the same intensity and at the same time as you train your body. As an athlete you can only achieve the impossible when being in balance with your body, mind and heart. Let's take the Olympic Games. All athletes standing at the starting line are close to the same level of performance. The one who meditates and is in perfect balance with him/herself therefore has a better chance to overcome possible obstacles.

Throughout my entire career I came to the following conclusion: the longer the race, the more you have to draw energy from your inner athlete. The outer athlete will fade and is going to knock on your head after four to six hours – "Hey, I am hurting here, I am tired. Just stop and rest for a moment!" You need to be able to control and calm your mind. Always be aware of your abilities and believe in your strengths and never let go of your focus towards the true goal.

During races I have often observed athletes' faces being stressed. It has been one of my keys to success never to show how my legs felt. I did this by having a relaxed face all the time. Don't tighten up and don't force it too hard. Let it happen, it's not just you! You have all the forces of the universe that will support you if you open up.

People have often asked me before a race: "Will you break the existing record?" But that's not the point! It's not about any records, it's about the best you can be! As long as I reached my full potential I would be happy at the finish. Not because of the time or place or record but because I was pleased with the performance I achieved. It's not about winning, it's not about money, it's about making constant progress and becoming a better person on the lasting journey.

Olivier Bernhard of Switzerland is a winner of 6 Ironman races,
3-time Duathlon World Champion and a triathlon coach

Introduction
By the Sri Chinmoy Marathon Team

The aim of this book is to bring an inner dimension to your current physical and mental training. Meditation is an adventurous journey to your Source. By discovering your Self, you will find an unlimited inner potential. This inner potential will enable you to go beyond your physical and mental limits.

While participating in a sport, qualities like concentration, determination and self-confidence can be developed. When you learn the art of meditation, you can also develop awareness, intense will-power and inner peace. It is like training your inner capacities, which can help you do extremely well in your sport.

There can be something profoundly meditative about sport. Exercise itself, if practised with the right focus, is a form of meditation and can be a meditative experience. The repetitive movement and regular breathing in endurance sports, such as running, swimming and cycling, help to induce a calm and reflective mind. Restless thoughts disappear and we feel at one with ourselves and with nature. While practising sport we enjoy a pure state of being, free from worries and anxieties. The joy and satisfaction experienced by athletes of any sport is similar to the joy and satisfaction of meditation. While the joy in sport is fleeting, the joy in meditation is infinite and everlasting.

In the past there was a golden link connecting the inner world of meditation with the outer world of sport. From ancient India this knowledge travelled to Japan and was preserved there for centuries by the Zen Buddhist monks from Mount Huei. Living examples of this golden link, these 'marathon monks' made running part of their spiritual discipline, believing that running led to enlightenment. They often covered hundreds of kilometres per week through the inhospitable mountains, clad only in a white robe and simple sandals. Their power of meditation kept them going and gave them an almost superhuman strength.

The art of meditation was developed mainly in the East. For example, in India the inner search for joy and truth had traditionally been given so much importance that for centuries the outer life was neglected because spirit and matter were mistakenly seen as separate existences. Not until the beginning of the 20th century, when the Indian spiritual leader and mystic Sri Aurobindo (1872–1950) revealed his philosophy of Integral Yoga*, was meditation brought out of isolation and integrated into an active and dynamic lifestyle. In the Sri Aurobindo Ashram (spiritual community) in South India, the teachings of meditation were combined with a Western-style education and the practice of sports such as soccer, basketball and track and field.

For twenty years Sri Chinmoy was a member of the Sri Aurobindo Ashram, where he became a top sprinter and decathlete. In 1964 he moved to New York City and became one of the first meditation masters who enthusiastically and wholeheartedly combined sport and meditation. For Sri Chinmoy, sport and meditation were complementary realities.

One of the cornerstones of Sri Chinmoy's philosophy is the concept of self-transcendence, the ability to go beyond one's perceived limitations in order to make constant progress. "It is only through progress," Sri Chinmoy says, "that we can become truly happy." Deep within us there is an inexhaustible source of cosmic energy that can be accessed through the power of meditation. This energy can be applied in all of our physical activities and will give a tremendous boost to our achievements.

At the age of 53 Sri Chinmoy began weightlifting. It was very inspiring to see him start a new sport at this age with such zeal and determination. With the progress he made in just a few months he amazed professional weightlifters and bodybuilders alike. Sri Chinmoy began by lifting forty pounds (18 kg), yet within five months, he was able to lift his own bodyweight of 155 pounds (70 kg) using just one arm. After only one year, he was able to lift 240 pounds (109 kg), more than one and a half times his body weight.

---

* *The term 'Yoga' here refers to the practice of the spiritual life. (See appendix)*

As a spiritual master, Sri Chinmoy demonstrated how the physical and the spiritual can go together. In his early years he meditated up to eight hours a day while also maintaining a regular daily training routine of many hours. Even when he was in his sixties and seventies, Sri Chinmoy regularly lifted weights for many hours a day in order to inspire people to conquer the age barrier and to never give up.

During his lifetime many world-class athletes met with Sri Chinmoy, athletes such as Jesse Owens, Carl Lewis, Muhammad Ali, Bill Pearl, Paul Tergat, Toshihiko Seko, Tegla Loroupe, Tatyana Lebedeva, Paula Radcliffe, Bill Rodgers, Steffi Graf, Monika Seles and Emil Zatopek. Nine-time Olympic champion Carl Lewis became one of Sri Chinmoy's closest friends. Sri Chinmoy accompanied Carl to three Olympic Games and encouraged Carl to feel that there are no limits to an athlete's capacity.

Although today's world-class athletes may have reached the current physical limits of the human body, the spiritual resources hidden deeper within still remain untapped. The inner training of our mind, heart and soul will enable us to enhance our physical performance beyond our imagination. Sri Chinmoy believed that many of today's world records can be broken by learning how to concentrate and meditate. In this respect Sri Chinmoy often spoke about the possibility of the sub two-hour marathon and the appropriate inner attitude and spiritual qualities required for it.

●●●

This book is not only for the serious athlete. Sri Chinmoy's words are meant for the beginner and the amateur as well. Everyone can transcend himself or herself, regardless of talent or skill. All that is needed is the urge to improve, the faith in one's own inner realities and the will to 'never give up'.

CHAPTER ONE

The Inner Athlete

*Where is the greatest victory?
The greatest victory lies in
Self-discovery.*

Body and Soul: From Ancient Times to Now

In sports we need energy, strength and dynamism. When we meditate, we make our mind calm and quiet. If inside us there is peace, then we will derive tremendous strength from our inner life. That is to say, if I have a peaceful moment, even for one second, that peace will come to me as solid strength in my sports, whether I am running or jumping or throwing. That strength is almost indomitable strength, whereas if we are restless, we do not have strength like that.

In our inner life if we have the strength of an elephant, then only in our outer life can we be peaceful. Meditation gives us inner strength. Once we have inner strength, we are bound to be successful in our outer life.

Most human beings negate the inner life. They feel that the inner life is not important as long as they can exist on earth. Again, there are a few who think that the outer life is not necessary. It is said that Indian teachers do not accept society

The inner athlete. *Sri Chinmoy at the start of a 100-metre dash in Pondicherry, India (circa 1950).*

as such. It is said that they do not care for the world but they care only for their spiritual life, that they like to be in the Himalayan caves and practise austerity and so forth. As long as they can get their own realisation, it is more than enough for them. But the philosophy that I have been taught from deep within is different. My philosophy says that we have to be in the world and we have to be for the world. We have to be like a boat. The boat is in the water, but the water does not enter into the boat. This is the boat that is taking us from ignorance to knowledge-shore. Also I would like to tell the world not to neglect the body-consciousness. I feel that the body must be kept fit.

In the absolutely ancient tradition in Vedic times and in the time of the Mahabharata* they practised archery and all sorts of things; they were physically strong. Then came an era for lethargy-prone people, so they separated spiritual-ity very nicely from the physical, the vital** and the mind. They created a big gap between the two and said, "If you are spiritual, you cannot do physical things, and if you are physically active, you cannot pray and meditate." But we say, "No, spirituality can be in the physical and the physical can be in the spiritual."

I wish to say that there should be a combination of the Indian spirit, which is calm, quiet and tranquil, and the Western spirit, which is dynamic. We have to take them as one. Matter is the pride of the West. Spirit is the pride of the East. Neither of the two can possess a complete satisfaction, for the former is in the dark about the potentialities of the spirit, and the latter about the cogency of matter. There can be no abiding happiness until matter and spirit are amalgamated into one reality.

Here we are on earth, in the physical body, and the Light we receive from our meditation must be expressed through the physical. The body-consciousness must not be neglected. The higher messages that we get from our meditation must have a channel for expression and the body is that channel.

A spiritual person has to give equal importance to both the body and the soul. If he pays attention only to the body, if he becomes physically strong but

---

* *Indian Epic*
** *'The vital' – the part of our being which houses emotional, dynamic and aggressive qualities.*
  (See appendix)

spiritually very weak, then for him there will be no peace of mind or inner happiness. If someone does not get any exercise at all, then the physical will remain unlit, lethargic and a real hindrance to the aspirant. If the physical consciousness does not aspire, it will remain separated from the soul. Then rest assured, you will never be able to achieve perfection. The physical has to aspire in its own way to increase its capacity so that it can hold light. So physical fitness and spirituality must go together. It is like having two legs. With one leg I cannot walk; I need two legs to reach my destination.

The body is like a temple, and the soul or inner reality is like the shrine inside the body-temple. If the temple does not have a shrine, then we cannot appreciate the temple. Again, if we do not keep the temple in good condition, then how can we take proper care of the shrine? We have to keep the body fit, and for this, running is of considerable help. If we are physically fit, then we will be more inspired to get up early in the morning to meditate. True, the inspiration to meditate comes from within, but if we do not have a stomach upset or headache or any other physical ailment, then it will be much easier for us to get up to pray and meditate. In this way the inner life is being helped by the outer life. Again, if I am inspired to get up early to meditate, then I will also be able to go out and run. Here we see that the outer life is being helped by the inner life.

The Outer Running and the Inner Running

The outer running is an extraordinary success on the mountain-summit. The inner running is an exemplary progress along Eternity's sunlit Road. Success is the ready and immediate acceptance of the challenges from difficulties untold. Progress is the soulful and grateful acceptance of the blessingful joy from prosperities unfathomed.

•●•

Both the outer running and the inner running are important. A marathon is twenty-six miles. Let us say that twenty-six miles is our ultimate goal. When we first take up running, we cannot run that distance. But by practising every day, we develop more stamina, speed, perseverance and so forth. Gradually we transcend our capacity and eventually we reach our goal.

We can say that our prayer and meditation is our inner running. If we pray and meditate every day, we increase our inner capacity. The body's capacity and the soul's capacity, the body's speed and the soul's speed, go together. The soul is running along Eternity's Road. The outer running reminds us of our inner running. In this way our body reminds us of something higher and deeper – the soul – which is dealing with Eternity, Infinity and Immortality. Running and physical fitness help us both in our inner life of aspiration* and in our outer life of activity.

The only difference between the outer running and the inner running is that in the inner running there is no set goal or destination. In the outer running, as soon as I have finished one hundred metres, let us say, the race is over. I may not win, but I have reached my goal. But in the inner running, we are Eternity's runner. Because we pray and meditate, we know that we have three friends: Eternity, Infinity and Immortality. Because we belong to Eternity, Infinity and Immortality, our journey is birthless and deathless; it has no beginning and no end. We have already started our journey and we are never going to end it. Along the way we may have certain temporary goals. But as soon as we reach these goals, they only become the starting point for new and higher goals.

 We run. We become.
We run in the outer world.
We become in the inner world.
We run to succeed.
We become to proceed.

---

* *Aspiration is the inner mounting cry of our soul for perfection and truth. (See appendix)*

At every moment we are running to become something great, sublime, divine and supreme. While we are becoming, we feel that we are in the process of reaching our ultimate Goal. But today's Goal is only the starting point for tomorrow's new dawn. At every moment we are transcending our previous achievements; we are transcending what we have and what we are.

Where is our Goal? It is not in the blue skies, it is not in the vast ocean, it is not in the distant desert – it is deep inside us, in the inmost recesses of our heart.* Our spiritual heart is infinitely larger than the world. The world grows and flows inside the spiritual heart. If we can feel that our aspiring heart is the living breath of the Supreme**, then we are bound to feel that our cherished goal is within, not without.

The Inner Runner

Every day, when morning dawns, we should feel that we have something new to accomplish. We are running and every day we are advancing. If we are aspiring, we are always in the process of running. When we start our journey in the morning, we should feel that today is the continuation of yesterday's journey; we should not take it as a totally new beginning. And tomorrow we should feel that we have travelled still another mile. Every day we should feel that we have travelled another mile. Then, we know one day that we will reach our Goal. Even if our speed decreases, we have to continue running and not give up on the way. When we reach our Goal we will see that it was worth the struggle.

Each individual on earth is running towards his destination. If the runner is wise, he will be very simple; he will wear only the basic, necessary garments, and not something very heavy or expensive which will draw the attention of the spectators. If the runner is wise, he will also be sincere. Sincerity means that he will yearn only for the goal and not be distracted by the flowers and fruits that he passes along the way. If the runner is sincere, he will run only in his own lane. He

---

* *The spiritual heart is an energy centre located in the centre of the chest. (See appendix)*
** *Sri Chinmoy preferred the term 'Supreme' instead of saying 'God' or 'Father'. (See appendix)*

will not enter into the lanes of others and disturb them. The wise runner will also be pure*. When we are pure, we see clearly with our inner vision that not only are we running toward the ultimate Goal, but the Goal itself is also running towards us.

When we run in the outer world, we have only a few competitors, and the competition will last for only a few hours. But in the inner world we have many competitors, and it may take a long time to defeat them. Our competitors in the inner world are fear, doubt, anxiety, depression, worry and similar forces that are all the time trying to rob us of our joy.

Try to be a runner, and try all the time to surpass and go beyond all that is bothering you and standing in your way. Be a real runner so that ignorance, limitation and imperfection will all drop far behind you in the race. If you carry inside you undivine elements like fear, doubt, anxiety, insecurity and so forth, that means you are carrying an extra weight and diminishing your capacity. A runner knows that if he carries extra weight, his opponents will defeat him.

When negative forces enter into your mind, just empty them out, cast them aside so that you can run the fastest. When the mind is calm and tranquil, then you can run the fastest without carrying a heavy load.

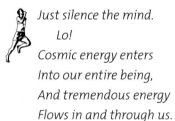

Just silence the mind.
Lo!
Cosmic energy enters
Into our entire being,
And tremendous energy
Flows in and through us.

---

* *Purity means to be free of imperfections such as doubt, insincerity, fear or jealousy. (See appendix)*

Inner Qualities of Swimming and Cycling

Swimming has its own symbolic value. The spiritual significance of water is consciousness. We are all eager to be in a good consciousness. As soon as we are in water, consciousness enters. So swimming has its own very special reality and divinity. While we are swimming, we can imagine that we are crossing from ignorance-sea into the sea of light and wisdom.

While we are cycling, we are reminding ourselves of evolution, of how the world is evolving in cycles. When we think of our planet, we think of a wheel turning; our life also is evolving like a wheel. So cycling reminds us of the process of evolution and of how everything goes in cycles. Once upon a time, in the hoary past, we lived in an era of truth. Now we are living in an era of falsehood. There was a time when truth reigned supreme, but now we see at every moment and every place that falsehood is reigning supreme. Our goal is to bring back again the golden age in which truth will be our inner guide and will reign supreme. So cycling reminds us of evolution, inner and outer. And in the process of evolution, our life-process, our life-energy – everything – is spinning so fast. The faster we can go, the sooner we will be able to have outer success and inner progress. And with our outer success and inner progress, we will be able to arrive at our goal infinitely faster than otherwise.

I love my great triathlon.
It shows my heart the God-Vision-Dawn.
I swim in the sea of silver light,
I cycle along the road of gold delight,
I run with the smile of the Beyond.
My inner cry: God-Treasure-Diamond!

Running and the Life-Game

Life and sports cannot be separated; they are one. As a matter of fact, life itself is a game. This game can be played extremely well, provided the player develops consciously or unconsciously the capacity to invoke the transcendental energy which is always manifested in action. In the life-game, each soul is running consciously or unconsciously toward the goal of inner perfection.

Spirituality is a one-way road that leads you to your goal. Once you have embarked on your journey, you cannot go back. The starting point is gone. Once evolution starts on any plane, you can not go back to the initial point.

Spirituality is an inner cry for the Source. Spirituality is an inner cry, an inner decision and an inner determination for perfection. What does it mean to be spiritual? To be spiritual is to be normal, natural and spontaneous. It means we long for perfection in our body, vital, mind and heart.

Searching for Our Source of Existence

If you have faith in the creation, then will you not look for the Creator? If you see that a wristwatch is giving the time correctly, then you can be satisfied with the wristwatch and go no further. But if you want to understand how the wristwatch operates, then will you not go to the watchmaker? Similarly, there are millions and billions of people on earth who are satisfied with the world as such. But again, there are some people who are not satisfied. Those who are not satisfied want to dive deep within and find the source or the cause of the suffering in this world. When they go to the Source, they see that it is all light and delight.

It depends on you. You can be satisfied with what you get. Then again, you can say, "Who is giving it to me?" Suppose Sunday was your best marathon and it gave you joy. You can say, "Now, who has given me this joy? Who has given me the capacity to run?" If you say that your own body, vital, mind and heart have given you the capacity, then who has given them the capacity? Somebody else has done it. Once we look for that somebody else, we see that He is none other than our own highest reality. A deer runs here and there searching for the source of the musk that it smells. But the musk is inside the deer itself. Now we are looking for someone. We feel that it is a third person. But when we see that person, we realise that it is only our selfsame reality in its highest form.

Where is the greatest victory? The greatest victory lies in self-discovery. *Atmanam Viddhi*: Know thyself. There can be no greater victory than to know oneself.

We are lumps of clay. But who has given the form to this clay? When we see a vessel, we know that somebody has made it. It did not just come out of the blue. We have to go to the Source. The earthen pot is not the ultimate reality. Somebody has shaped it. That somebody is the one we are searching for. We can call it the Ultimate Reality, we can call it God, or we can call it by any other name. But we have to give credit to someone. When we go to that somebody, after a long search, we see that the one we sought was our own highest Self. The highest in us was being sought by the lowest. We just climb up from the foot of the tree to the highest branch.

Something within us, an inner urge, inspires us to go outside and run. Who gave us that inner urge? Again, we have to go to the Source. The questions never end until we dive deep within. Then all questions are answered. But it does not happen overnight. As you know, you had to practise for months or years to complete the marathon. Similarly, we have to pray and meditate for years if we want to cover long inner distances. It is a lifelong process.

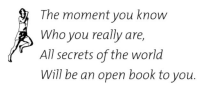

The moment you know
Who you really are,
All secrets of the world
Will be an open book to you.

Self-Transcendence: Going Beyond

Today's goal has to be transcended tomorrow. Today's goal is the foundation-stone. Every moment we have to transcend ourselves and, while transcending, deep within us we shall cherish the message of perfection. Self-transcendence is the song of constant inner progress and constant outer progress.

I do not have any set goal; my goal is self-transcendence. I always try to transcend myself. I do not compete with the rest of the world. I compete only with myself, and I try to become a better human being. This is my ultimate goal.

The world cares for speed, so we have to prove that we are absolutely the fastest. How I wish all human beings would run faster than the fastest, with unimaginable speed, towards Eternity's ever-transcending Goal. Once we reach the highest transcendental Height with our fastest speed and consciously begin serving our Supreme Pilot* at every moment, at that time we can and we shall create an absolutely new creation. At that time there will be only one reality, one song: the song of self-transcendence. There will be no boxing ring where might is right. There will be no destruction. In order to prove our supremacy, we will only have to transcend ourselves the way the Absolute Supreme is transcending Himself. The supreme secret or goal will be to transcend our own capacities. We will not try to defeat others. We will try only to constantly transcend ourselves. In this way we will get supreme satisfaction and offer supreme satisfaction to the inner world and to the outer world.

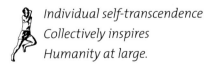

Individual self-transcendence
Collectively inspires
Humanity at large.

---

*   *Our inner guide, our own highest Self who guides us. (See appendix)*

↑

Crossing the English Channel *represents one of the great feats of self-transcendence in the swimming world.*

When I reach a certain standard, if it is the Will of the Supreme that I reach only that particular height, then I give up. Otherwise, I never give up. I continue, continue, continue, all the time trying to transcend my previous limit. My goal is always to go beyond, beyond, beyond. There are no limits to our capacity, because we have the infinite Divine within us, and the Supreme is always transcending His own Reality-Existence. So my only goal is progress, and there is no end to our progress.

When you come to a particular standard, you have to say, "Is there anything more I can do?" Then do it.

We always limit ourselves just because we do not feel that there is Somebody deep within us to inspire us, to guide us, to mould us, to shape us and to take us to an ever-transcending Reality. When we think of ourselves, we think of ourselves with very limited capacities. When we are in the body, mind or vital, everything is so limited. We are caged in a prison cell. But when we are in the soul, we are dealing with the limitless.

What the Supreme is trying to do is to let the finite in us, the little brother in us, try to follow the big brother in us, which is the soul. So our outer life is trying to run side by side with our inner life. Our inner life is flowing eternally in and through us, and we are trying to bring to the fore its boundless capacities. When one of my students runs one thousand miles or when I am drawing three million birds, at that time we are trying to enter into the unlimited Source, which we all have within us and which we actually are. We are trying to bring our own limitless capacity to the fore.

 We have to believe in a higher Power.
Only by believing in a higher Power
Can we go beyond and beyond
Our limited, human capacity.

Self-transcendence brings us the message of happiness. Self-transcendence gives us joy in boundless measure. Each time we surpass our previous achievements, we get joy.

There are quite a few ways to transcend ourselves, but the two main ways are the humility-way and the awareness-way. We try to cultivate humility, true and soulful humility. It is through humility that we acquire the power of receptivity. When we have the power of receptivity, at that time Peace, Light and Bliss in boundless measure descend from above, and with no difficulty we can embody these divine attributes.

Inner Peace: Our Protection and Treasure

In the outer life you cannot have peace unless and until you have first established peace in your inner life.

No price is too great to pay for inner peace. Peace is the harmonious control of life. It is vibrant with life-energy. It is a power that easily transcends all our worldly knowledge. Yet it is not separate from our earthly existence. If we open the right avenues within, this peace can be felt here and now.

Peace is eternal. It is never too late to have peace. Time is always ripe for that. We can make our life truly fruitful if we are not cut off from our Source, which is the Peace of Eternity.

The greatest misfortune that can come to a human being is to lose his inner peace. No outer force can rob him of it. It is his own thoughts, his own actions, that rob him of it.

Our greatest protection lies not in our material achievements and resources. All the treasure of the world is emptiness to our divine soul. Our greatest protection lies in our soul's communion with the all-nourishing and all-fulfilling Peace. Our soul lives in Peace and lives for Peace. If we live a life of peace, we are ever enriched and never impoverished. Unhorizoned is our inner peace; like the boundless sky, it encompasses all. Long have we struggled, much have we suffered, far have we travelled. But the face of peace is still hidden from us. We can discover it if ever the train of our desires loses itself in the Will of the Lord Supreme.

Inner Peace Gives Us Strength for Daily Challenges

In our ordinary life, no matter how much material wealth we have, no matter how much outer authority we can exercise, we shall not be satisfied. What we want from our lives is satisfaction – nothing more, nothing less. This satisfaction we are bound to achieve, provided we dive deep within and approach the outer world from the inner world.

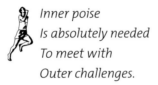

Inner poise
Is absolutely needed
To meet with
Outer challenges.

Think that you are standing in front of the sea. The surface of the sea is very dynamic; it is all waves and surges. But the bottom of the sea is all calmness and peace. You can identify yourself with the surface of the sea and also with its depths. Similarly, you can identify with both the outer world and the inner world. While looking at the outer life, you see dynamism and speed. But even while you are looking at the outer life you can dive into the inner life, where it is all peace and inner poise. If you dive within and become inseparably one with inner peace, then easily you can bring inner peace to the fore so that it inundates your outer life.

If we meditate soulfully in the morning and receive peace for only one minute, that one minute of peace will permeate our whole day. In the morning, when you pray and meditate, feel that you have gained real wealth in the form of peace. As you keep your money inside your pocket, even so you can keep your peace inside your heart. With money-power you can buy whatever you want. Similarly, the spiritual power that you get from prayer and meditation is a real power. When people are quarrelling, fighting, or behaving undivinely, just bring forward the inner peace and poise which you have kept inside your heart. Surcharge yourself once more with inner peace. The power of inner peace is infinitely more solid and concrete than any outer disturbance anybody can create on earth. Your inner peace can easily devour the irritation caused by others. So before we go to work, before we enter into the hustle and bustle of the world, we should pray and meditate for a few minutes in order to inundate our inner life with peace, light and bliss. If we are not guided by our inner thoughts, inner goodwill, inner strength, then we will be nowhere in the outer life. The inner life, the inner practicality, must guide the outer life, and not the other way around. It is not that the outer life will have a separate existence. No! The life-breath of the outer life has to come from the inner life.

Peace itself is strength. If you have inner peace, you will have joy and delight when you enter into the outer world. The outer world can be under your control when you have peace of mind. Wherever you go, you will make your own peace. In great power, there is quietude.

Before you enter into
The whirlpool of activities,
Calm your mind.
Then success and progress
Will be all yours.

CHAPTER TWO

Meditation and Concentration

In the heart of action
Is the silence of meditation
And in the heart of meditation
Is the dynamism of action.

What is Meditation?

Meditation means conscious self-expansion. Meditation means the recognition or the discovery of one's own true self. It is through meditation that we transcend limitation, bondage and imperfection. Meditation is dynamism on the inner planes of consciousness. If we want to achieve anything, either in our inner life or our outer life, then the help of meditation is of paramount importance. When we meditate, what we actually do is enter into the deeper part of our being. At that time, we are able to bring to the fore the wealth that we have deep within us.

Meditation shows us how we can aspire for something and, at the same time, how we can achieve it. If we practise meditation daily, then we can rest assured that the problems of our life, inner and outer, are solved. Meditation simplifies our outer life and energises our inner life, meditation gives us a natural and spontaneous life.

During meditation what we actually do is enter into a vacant, calm, still, silent mind. We go deep within and approach our true existence, which is our soul. When we live in the soul, we feel that we are actually meditating spontaneously. At that time, we see that our inner existence is surcharged with peace and tranquillity.

Meditation is like going to the bottom of the sea, where everything is calm and tranquil. On the surface there may be a multitude of waves, but the sea is not affected below. In its deepest depths, the sea is all silence. When we start meditating, first we try to reach our own inner existence – that is to say, the bottom of the sea. Then, when the waves come from the outside world, we are not affected. Fear, doubt, worry and all the earthly turmoils will just wash away, because inside us is solid peace. Thoughts cannot touch us, because our mind is all peace, all silence, all oneness. Like fish in the sea, they jump and swim but leave no mark on the water. Like birds flying in the sky, they leave no trace behind them. So when we are in our highest meditation we feel that we are the sea, and the animals in the sea cannot affect us. We feel that we are the sky, and all the birds flying past cannot affect us. Our mind is the sky and our heart is the infinite sea. This is meditation.

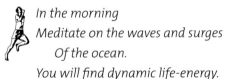

In the morning
Meditate on the waves and surges
    Of the ocean.
You will find dynamic life-energy.

In the evening
Meditate on the deep vastness
    Of the ocean.
You will feel Infinity's peace.

The ocean embodies indomitable power and energy, but at the same time, silence and
peace. Both aspects must work in harmony if we are to achieve anything in our life.

Meditation is something wide and vast that ultimately expands into the Infinite.
When we meditate, we throw ourselves into a vast expanse, into an infinite sea of
peace and bliss, or we welcome the infinite Vast into us. Prayer rises; meditation
spreads. Meditation is constantly growing and expanding into peace, light and delight.

Meditation does not mean just sitting quietly for five or ten minutes. It
requires conscious effort. The mind has to be made calm and quiet. At the same
time, it has to be vigilant so as not to allow any distracting thoughts or desires to
enter. When we can make the mind calm and quiet, we will feel that a new creation is dawning inside us. When the mind is vacant and tranquil and our whole

existence becomes an empty vessel, our inner being can invoke infinite peace, light and bliss to enter into the vessel and fill it.

Meditation means conscious awareness of our source. When we meditate, we consciously try to go to the source, which is all perfection. Our source is God, our source is truth, our source is light. Meditation takes us to our source, where there is no imperfection, no ailment. And where is the source? It is within us. One who has inner awareness has free access to infinite Truth and everlasting Joy, and he will be able to control his outer life. What gives us inner awareness? Meditation.

Each individual seeker* has an intimate friend, a constant companion, a friend who is always with him. Who is his best friend? The Real in him. The Real in him is the eternal seeker, who has an eternal longing for Truth, Peace, Light and Bliss in abundant measure.

The Soul's Evolution

Through meditation the soul becomes fully aware of its evolution in its eternal journey. Before taking human incarnation, the soul gets an inner message about its divine purpose on earth. It is fully conscious of its mission. But during our lifetime, the workings of the physical mind may sometimes cover up the divine inspiration of the soul and its true purpose. Then the mission of the soul cannot come forward. Only if we aspire with the mind, heart, and soul can we learn the purpose of our existence here on earth.

The athlete must sincerely feel that he has a soul and not just think so because someone has said it is true. Many people do not have direct access even to their heart, so how can they have access to their soul? It is through meditation, continuous and regular meditation, that we can feel the presence of the soul and eventually see the soul. But even if we do not see the soul, if we just feel the presence of the soul inside the depth of our heart, then gradually we can bring its light into the vital, mind and physical. But first we have to know that the soul exists. It must not be just mental belief but a real psychic experience.

---

* *The term 'seeker' refers to our inner search for our true Self. (See appendix)*

When the soul's will-power is utilised, it is like a huge wave in the sea. Immediately it inundates the entire consciousness. Once the soul's will is expressed, we are bound to feel that our inner consciousness is inundated with divine energy, inner joy, inner delight, inner power and inner confidence. Everything negative is swept away by the surge of the soul's force.

Peace of Mind: a Positive Force

When we meditate, we try to become a perfect channel for the positive force. The positive force is light, and the negative force is darkness. The positive force is love, not hatred. The positive force is belief, not disbelief. At each moment in our life the positive force helps us because it takes us consciously to our destination, which is perfection.

If our mind is calm and quiet, if our vital is dynamic, if our body is conscious of what it is doing, then we are inside the palace of satisfaction, where there can be no disease, no suffering, no imperfection, no obstruction to our abiding peace, abiding light, abiding satisfaction. Meditation is a means; it is a way; it is a path. If we walk along this path, then we reach our destination, which is all perfection.

When we meditate, what result do we get in the outer life? We make our mind calm and quiet. It is almost impossible for most human beings to have peace of mind. He who does not have peace of mind is a veritable beggar; he is like a monkey in a human body. He has no satisfaction. But if we get peace of mind for one fleeting second, we feel we have accomplished a lot in life. When we have peace of mind, our vital and our body become peaceful; and where there is peace there is no disharmony. It is only in the world of anxiety, dissatisfaction, tension and confusion that there is disharmony. Otherwise, there would be no ailments. When there is real harmony, the sufferings of human life come to an end.

Meditation is not an escape. Meditation is the acceptance of life in its totality with a view to transforming it for the highest manifestation of the divine Truth here on earth.

Concentration-Power

Without concentration we can not be successful in our sport. For those who wish to enter into meditation, we must first master the art of concentration power.

*Five days before a record-breaking solo climb of the Eiger North Face, the Swiss mountain climber **Ueli Steck** spoke in an interview about how in free climbing and speed climbing concentration and the focus on the moment are absolutely essential.*

I am always looking for goals that are challenging me and take all my attention. I go one-pointed towards the goal: I am not just climbing – this is not my way. I really want to reach the goal.

"My concentration is also my life insurance. In critical moments, I concentrate very hard on what goes positive, never on what is going wrong. There is always a solution.

"While climbing I never look down. To my goal it does not go down, it only goes up! Up there, on the very top, there is the goal. To get there, I go on a path, and what counts on that path is only the 'Now'. Thoughts that precede are wasted thoughts, because they are unnecessary. The future is coming. Very often it depends on the present. The more conscious we are of doing the right thing at the present, the better looks the future. It's all about the Now! Nothing other than the moment.

"From this total concentration in the here and now, a few times I experienced watching myself climbing, seeing that my body is just an instrument. Once it happened when I was climbing the difficult route 'Excalibur' in the Swiss Alps...

*"**Here and now**". Ueli Steck free solo climbing the "Excalibur" pillar, a classic route in the Swiss Alps. (Photo © Robert Boesch)*

↑

Focusing on the motto "Compete only with yourself", Ueli Steck set in 2008 a new speed record on the Eiger North Face in 2 h 47 min, which he transcended in 2015 to an amazing 2 h 23 min. (Photo © Robert Boesch)

...free solo. It was as if I were watching myself from the outside. I saw my body climbing and thought, 'Wow, he is doing well!' That is the time when concentration becomes meditation; it is indescribable. Only the moment and myself, the inhaling and the exhaling.

"Reaching the top I felt joy. Extreme joy! Joy in the knowledge that the sky was much bigger and much wider than yesterday."

—**Ueli Steck**

Concentration means inner vigilance and alertness. There are thieves all around us and within us. Fear, doubt, worry and anxiety are inner thieves that are trying to steal our inner poise and peace of mind. When we learn how to concentrate, it is very difficult for these forces to enter into us. If doubt enters into our mind, the power of concentration will tear doubt to pieces. If fear enters into our mind, the power of concentration will chase away our fear.

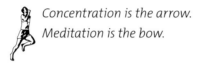 *Concentration is the arrow.*
Meditation is the bow.

When we concentrate, we do not allow any thought to enter into our mind, whether it is divine or undivine, earthly or heavenly, good or bad. The entire mind is focused totally on a particular object or subject. If we are concentrating on the petal of a flower, we have to feel that nothing else exists in the entire world but us and the petal. We will look neither forward nor backward, upward nor inward. We will just try to pierce the object that we are focusing on with our one-pointed concentration. Concentration is like an arrow entering into the target. But it is not an aggressive way of looking into a thing or entering into an object. Far from it! This concentration comes directly from the heart, or more precisely, from the soul. We call it the soul's indomitable will or will-power.

Very often I hear aspirants say that they cannot concentrate for more than five minutes. After five minutes they get a headache or they feel that their head is on fire. Why? It is because the power of their concentration is coming from the intellectual mind or, you can say, the disciplined mind. The mind knows that it must not wander; that much knowledge the mind has. But if the mind is to be utilised properly, in an illumined way, then the light of the soul has to come into it. When the light of the soul has entered into the mind, it is extremely easy for us to concentrate on something for two or three hours, or for as long as we

Concentration
Is the midday sun-power.
As soon as you see this sun,
Your entire being is flooded
With strength.

Meditation
Is the moonlit peace.
As soon as you see this moon,
You can feel peace within
And peace without.

Why am I so tired?
I am tired
Not because I work very hard,
Not because I sleep too little,
But because I think too much.

want. During this time there can be no thoughts or doubts or fears. No negative forces can enter into our mind if it is surcharged with the soul's light.

So when we concentrate, we try to feel that the power of concentration is coming from the heart centre and then going up to the third eye*. The physical heart is tiny, but the spiritual heart, which is our true home, is vaster than the universe. The heart centre is where the soul is located. When we think of our soul, at this time we should not form any specific idea of it or think what it looks like. We should just think of it as God's representative, as boundless Light and Delight. So this Light comes from our heart and passes through our third eye, and then it takes us into the object of our concentration and we have our identification with it. The final stage of concentration is to discover the hidden ultimate truth in the object of concentration.

We should concentrate for a few minutes each day before entering into meditation. At that time we are acting like a runner who has to clear the track; we see if there are any obstacles and then remove them. Once concentration has removed the obstacles and we begin

* *The eye of inner vision. (See appendix)*

meditating, we can run very fast. Inwardly we become like an express train that only stops at the final destination. One-pointed concentration is the pathfinder for a deeper meditative consciousness.

Meditation: The Mind and the Heart

No matter which path you follow for meditation, the first and foremost task is to try to make the mind calm and quiet. If the mind is constantly roaming, if it is all the time a victim of merciless thoughts, then you will make no progress whatsoever. The mind has to be made calm and quiet so that when the light descends from above, you can be fully conscious of it.

How will you make the mind calm and quiet? The mind has its own power, and right now this power is stronger than your present eagerness and determination to meditate. But if you can get help from your heart, then gradually you will be able to control your mind. The heart, in turn, gets constant assistance from the soul, which is all light and all power.

You are constantly bothered by thoughts because you are trying to meditate inside your mind. The very nature of the mind is to welcome thoughts – good thoughts, bad thoughts, divine thoughts, undivine thoughts. If you meditate in the mind, you will be able to meditate for perhaps five minutes, and out of that five minutes, for one minute you may meditate very powerfully. First you get joy and satisfaction, but then you may feel a barren desert. If you meditate in the heart, a day will come when you start getting satisfaction. If you meditate in the heart, you are meditating where the soul is. True, the light, the consciousness of the soul permeates the whole body, but there is a specific place where the soul resides most of the time, and that is in the heart. I am not speaking of the human heart, the physical heart, which is just another organ. I am speaking of the pure heart, the spiritual heart. The spiritual heart is located in the centre of the chest, in the centre of our existence.

When you are trying to make your mind calm and quiet, you are concentrating. When you are successful in chasing away all thoughts that disturb your mind sooner or later your inner self will automatically come to the fore and stand right in front of you like a blazing sun clearing away the veil of clouds. Right now the inner sun is overcast with clouds: thoughts, ideas, doubts, fears and so forth. Take the mind as a monkey or an unruly child. As many times as it comes to you, chase it away or deliberately place your conscious awareness on something else. If you allow it to distract you, it will gain strength and continue to torture you. During your meditation your mind may resist and obstruct you, but you have to feel that you have something superior to the mind, and that is your heart. Just throw the mind and all its possessions into the heart.

Remain always in the sunshine of your heart until its illumining rays have also flooded your mind.

You must not think that when there is nothing in your mind, you will become a fool or act like an idiot. This is not true. If you can keep your mind calm and quiet for ten or fifteen minutes, a new world will dawn within you. This is the root of all spiritual progress. Right now you can make your mind calm and quiet for only a few seconds, or for a minute, but if you can maintain your calmness, poise and tranquillity for half an hour or even for fifteen minutes, I assure you that inside your tranquillity a new world with tremendous divine light and power will grow.

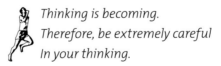

Thinking is becoming.
Therefore, be extremely careful
In your thinking.

   The mind is not necessary for meditation, because thinking and meditating are absolutely different things. When we meditate, we do not think at all. The aim of meditation is to free ourselves from all thought. Thought is like a dot on a blackboard. Whether it is good or bad, it is there. Only if there is no thought whatsoever can we grow into the highest reality. Even in profound meditation thoughts can come in, but not in the highest, deepest meditation. In the highest meditation, there will be only light.

Even reflection, which is a quiet kind of introspective thinking, is far from the disciplined vastness of meditation. The moment we start thinking, we play with limitation and bondage. Our thoughts, no matter how sweet or delicious at the moment, are painful and destructive in the long run because they limit and bind us.

There is a vast difference between what you can get from the mind and what you can get from the heart. The mind is limited; the heart is unlimited. When you meditate on the heart, you feel a sense of delight, a sense of oneness with something vast and infinite. In the heart there is infinite Light, Peace and Bliss. If you concentrate on the mind, you will not get what you want, because you have gone to the wrong place. With the mind you only divide yourself. The mind may try to do something and immediately the body or the vital may try to prevent it. But if the heart wants to do something, no matter how difficult, it will be done. If the mind gets no satisfaction when it tries something, it just says that there is no reality there and gives up. But when the heart does not get satisfaction, it feels that it has not done the thing properly. So it tries again, and continues trying until satisfaction dawns at last.

Let us not be satisfied with the things that we get very easily. Let us cry for something which is more difficult to get, but which is infinite and everlasting. If you get something from the mind, tomorrow doubt may come and tell you that it is not real. But once you get something from the heart you will never be able to doubt it or forget it. An experience on the psychic plane can never be erased from the heart.

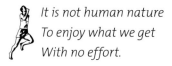
It is not human nature
To enjoy what we get
With no effort.

The ABCs of Meditation

When you do not give countless outer things your attention, you will see that truth is looking right at you and giving you the strength to discipline your life.

The best way to meditate is to sit cross-legged on a small cushion or rug. The spine and the neck must be kept erect. If it is not possible for some of you to sit that way, then please try, if you are sitting on a chair, to sit with your entire back straight and erect.

If you want to meditate at home, please try to keep a sacred place, a corner of your room, absolutely pure and sanctified. And please wear clean and light clothes. In order to have the utmost purity, it is extremely helpful to bathe before meditation, but if you are unable to take a bath or a shower before sitting down to meditate, you should at least wash your face and your feet. If possible, please burn incense at the time of your meditation, and place one flower, any flower, in front of you. The physical flower that you have in front of you reminds you of the inner flower. Its colour, its fragrance and its pure consciousness gives you a little inspiration.

It is the same with using candles during meditation. When you see the outer flame, then immediately you feel that the flame in your inner being is also climbing high, higher, highest.

Preparation and Posture

Meditation is like running. If you run stiffly, you get nowhere. You must be relaxed; the body has to be relaxed. But if you go to the extreme, then you become complacent.

Some seekers like to meditate while lying down, but I wish to say that this is not at all advisable for the beginner, nor even for those who have been meditating for several years. It is only for the most advanced seekers and for realised souls. Others who try to meditate while lying down will enter into the world of sleep or into a kind of inner drift or doze. Furthermore, while you are lying down, your breathing is not as satisfactory as it is when you are in a sitting position, since it is not conscious or controlled.

When you meditate, you have to be absolutely dynamic. Do not allow sleepiness to enter into you. The best thing is to breathe in deeply a few times before you meditate and make your whole body energetic. Your dynamic energy will help you enter into meditation. Or you can jog a little. If possible, take a small quantity of hot juice or hot milk before you enter your meditation. Then your whole system will be attuned with the divine energy, and this divine energy will take you to the proper place of meditation in your inner consciousness.

There are some Indian *asanas* that can offer a fresh supply of energy to the nerves, and to a certain extent the muscle-power can be increased by taking these exercises. These exercises, called Hatha Yoga, also relax the body and bring peace of mind for a short period. If someone is physically very restless and cannot stay still for more than a second, then these exercises will definitely help.

People often ask me if they should meditate with their eyes open. In ninety out of one hundred cases, those who keep their eyes closed during meditation fall asleep. For five minutes they meditate, and then for fifteen minutes they remain in the world of sleep. There is no dynamic energy, but only lethargy, complacency and a kind of restful, sweet sensation. So it is best to meditate with the eyes half open and half closed.

The Hour of Meditation

The best hour for meditation, according to Indian seers, sages and spiritual Masters, is between three and four o'clock in the morning. That is called *Brahma Muhurta*, the time of the Brahman, the best time. But here in the West, if you go to bed late, the best hour for you is five-thirty or six in the morning. The precise hour is to be settled according to the individual case and the individual capacity.

Whether you meditate in the morning or the evening, it is of paramount importance to have a fixed time for your meditation. If you meditate in the morning, you will find that your meditation will be most fruitful. Before the sun rises, the earth-consciousness is not yet agitated. The world has not yet entered into its daily turmoil. Nature is calm and quiet and will help you meditate. Once the day dawns, Mother Earth becomes divinely energetic or undivinely restless. These restless qualities of the world do not have to enter into you, but usually they will. When people move around, immediately their vibration enters into you, no matter where you are. The air, the light, everything around you becomes permeated with the vibration of human activity and human anxieties. The world is standing in front of you like a roaring lion. How can you enter into your highest meditation in front of a roaring lion? But if you can meditate before the world awakens, when the cosmos is still and people around you are taking rest, then you will be able to have a deeper meditation. So anything that is most significant, anything that is momentous in your life, you should always try to do in the small hours of the morning.

 Do not depend on tomorrow.
Do not depend even on today.
Just depend on now,
This very moment.

If you cannot meditate in the morning, the evening is the next best time, because in the evening at least the atmosphere is becoming calm and peaceful. At noon nature is wild and restless, so your meditation may not be very deep or intense. But in the evening nature is preparing to rest and it does not disturb you. When you meditate in the evening, you can look at the setting sun and try to feel that you have become totally one with cosmic nature. You can feel that you have played your part during the day most satisfactorily and, like the sun, you are going to retire.

Your morning and evening meditations can be for a longer time, for fifteen minutes or half an hour, whereas your noon meditation can be as short as five or ten minutes. If it is not possible to feed your soul three times a day, then please feed it at least once.

It is better to meditate well just once a day in the morning than to sit five or six times a day with your eyes closed and just have pleasant thoughts drifting through your head.

Eating before Meditation

It is not good to meditate just after eating a large meal. The body has thousands of subtle spiritual nerves. These nerves become heavy after a big meal and will not permit you to have the highest type of meditation. The body will be heavy, the consciousness will be heavy, the nerves will be heavy, and your meditation will not be good. When you meditate properly, you feel that your whole existence, like a bird, is flying high, higher, highest. But when your consciousness is heavy, you cannot go up.

The major cords* – *Ida, Pingala* and *Sushumna* – find it extremely difficult to allow the cosmic energy to pass through them if the body has just taken a full meal. So it is always advisable to meditate on an empty stomach. At least two hours should elapse between your meal and the time that you sit down to meditate. But again, if you are really pinched with hunger when you go to meditate, your meditation will not be satisfactory. Your hunger, like a monkey, will constantly bother you. In that case, it is advisable to have just a glass of milk or juice before meditating. This will not ruin your meditation.

Diet

When we eat meat, the aggressive animal consciousness enters into us. Our nerves become agitated and restless, and this can interfere with our meditation. If a seeker does not stop eating meat, generally he does not get subtle experiences or subtle visions. The mild qualities of fruits and vegetables help us to establish, in our inner life as well as in our outer life, the qualities of sweetness, softness, simplicity and purity. If we are vegetarians, this helps our inner being to strengthen its own existence. Inwardly, we are praying and meditating; outwardly,

---

* *The streams of subtle energy that flow through the body. (See appendix)*

the food we are taking from Mother Earth is helping us too, giving us not only energy but also aspiration.

Some people feel that it is meat that gives them strength. But if they go deep within, they may discover that it is their own idea about meat that is giving them strength. One can change that idea and feel that it is not meat but the spiritual energy pervading one's body that gives one strength. That energy comes from meditation as well as from proper nourishment. The strength that one can get from aspiration and meditation is infinitely more powerful than the strength one can get from meat.

CHAPTER THREE

Concentration and Meditation Exercises

Outer endurance
Helps him meditate longer.
Inner peace of mind
Helps him run farther.

Proper Breathing

Proper breathing is very important in meditation. When breathing, try to breathe in as slowly and quietly as possible, so that if somebody placed a tiny thread in front of your nose it would not move at all. And when you breathe out, try to breathe out even more slowly than when you breathed in. If possible, leave a short pause between the end of your first exhalation and the beginning of your second inhalation. If you can, hold your breath for a few seconds. But if it is difficult, do not do it. Never do anything that will harm your organs or respiratory system.

Each time you breathe in, try to feel that you are bringing into your body peace, infinite peace. The opposite of peace is restlessness. When you breathe out, try to feel that you are expelling the restlessness within you and also the

41

restlessness that you see all around you. When you breathe this way, you will find restlessness leaving you. After practising this for a few times, please try to feel that you are breathing in power from the universe. And when you exhale, feel that all your fear is coming out of your body. After doing this a few times, try to feel that what you are breathing in is joy, infinite joy, and what you are breathing out is sorrow, suffering and melancholy.

There is another thing that you can also try. Feel that you are breathing in not air but cosmic energy. Feel that tremendous cosmic energy is entering into you with each breath and that you are going to use it to purify your body, vital, mind and heart. Feel that there is not a single place in your body that is not being occupied by the flow of cosmic energy. It is flowing like a river inside you, washing and purifying your whole being. Then, when you start to breathe out, feel that you are breathing out all the rubbish inside you. Anything inside your system that you call undivine, anything that you do not want to claim as your own, feel that you are exhaling. It is most important that this breathing be done in a very conscious way, not in a mechanical way. Otherwise, it will not be effective. If you practise this method of breathing, you will soon see its results. In the beginning you will have to use your imagination, but after a while you will see and feel that it is not imagination at all but reality. If you can breathe this way for five minutes every day, you will be able to make very fast progress.

→

Finding the inner wealth. Sri Chinmoy demonstrates meditation.

Prana: the Life-Energy

Prana is a Sanskrit word which means breath, life-breath or life-energy. This life-energy is not something material or physical which can be seen by the scientists or doctors, but it is indispensable to life. The source of prana is the Supreme. Prana is as important in our life as *Atman,* which is the soul or Self.

Prana is a cosmic Force or a cosmic Energy which operates in the physical body. Human life has a short span in which the prana lasts for forty, sixty or eighty years. But the cosmic Energy in its own sphere lasts for eternity. There is a connecting link between the cosmic Energy, which is infinite, and the prana, as this energy is called when it enters into our physical body. This link is the soul. The soul and the prana work together. It is the soul which calls the prana into the physical body for a short span of years. Then when it is God's Will, the connection breaks between the cosmic Energy and the prana enclosed in the physical frame. At that time we lose the body and die.

When we meditate, if we can become conscious of our breathing, it will help us to become conscious of the great divine Breath, of which we are the instruments. When we start to meditate, if the flow of prana is spontaneous, steady and unobstructed, then the inner being is in a position to bring forward the inner wealth and make the outer personality feel, fulfil and realise the Highest.

Creating Energy with Pranayama

Another technique you can try is alternate breathing *(pranayama)*. This is done by pressing the right nostril closed with the thumb and taking in a long breath through the left nostril. As you breathe in, repeat 'Supreme' once. Then hold your breath for four counts repeating 'Supreme' four times. And finally release your right nostril, press your left nostril closed with your fourth finger and release your breath to the count of two – that is, two repetitions of 'Supreme'. Then do it the opposite way, starting with the left nostril pressed closed. In this system, when you breathe in, it does not have to be done quietly. Even if you make noise, no harm. But of course, these exercises should not be done in public or where other people are trying to meditate in silence.

If you can practise this exercise, the benefits will be unimaginable. But do not do it mechanically. Concentrate while you are breathing, and you are bound to feel that you are breathing in divine energy.

You should not practise one-four-two breathing for more than four or five minutes, and you should not do alternate breathing more than a few times. If you do it twenty or forty or fifty times, heat will rise from the base of your spine and enter into your head, creating tension and a headache. It is like eating too much. Eating is good, but if you eat voraciously, it will upset your stomach. This inner heat acts the same way. If you draw it up beyond your capacity, then instead of giving you a peaceful mind, it will give you an arrogant, turbulent and destructive mind. Later, when you have developed your inner capacity, you can do this alternate breathing for ten or fifteen minutes.

Concentration Exercises

As a general rule, you should start with concentration for a few months at least. Once you have learned to concentrate, then meditation becomes easy. But even when you are able to meditate, it is a good idea to concentrate for a few minutes before you start your daily meditation.

You cannot expect immediate results. The farmer sows the seed and then he waits; he never expects the crop to spring forth all at once. It takes a few weeks or a few months to germinate.

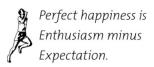 *Perfect happiness is Enthusiasm minus Expectation.*

The Thumb

When you concentrate, you have to feel that nothing exists except the thing that you are concentrating upon. When you concentrate, try to forget the rest of the world: what is within you, around you, before you, above you, below you. Concentrate on only one object. If you want to concentrate on the tip of your thumb, start with imagination. Imagine that your only possession is your thumb. There is nothing else which you can claim as your own. The rest of the body does not belong to you – only the thumb. If you want to concentrate on the tip of your nose, feel that you are the possessor of only your nose; you are not the possessor of your eyes, your ears, your mouth, your limbs. If you begin to think of something else, feel that you are entering into foreign territory. In this way you will develop your power of concentration.

You are at liberty to choose any part of your body to concentrate on, but try to use some part which you feel as your very own. And do not concentrate on your arm or your hand or your leg. Take a very small part of your body, the eye or the nose or the fingertip. The smaller the better for concentration.

The Dot

If you want to develop the power of concentration, then here is another exercise you can try. First wash your face and eyes properly with cold water. Then make a black dot on the wall at eye level. Stand facing the dot, about ten inches away, and concentrate on it. After a few minutes, try to feel that when you are breathing in, your breath is actually coming from the dot, and that the dot is also breathing in, getting its breath from you. Try to feel that there are two persons: you and the black dot. Your breath is coming from the dot and its breath is coming from you.

My Heart-Friend

Just as you can concentrate on the tip of your finger, or on a candle or any other material object, you can also concentrate on your heart. You may close your eyes or look at a wall, but all the time you are thinking of your heart as a dear friend. When this thinking becomes most intense, when it absorbs your entire attention,

then you have gone beyond ordinary thinking and entered into concentration. You cannot look physically at your spiritual heart, but you can focus all your attention on it. Then gradually the power of your concentration enters into the heart and takes you completely out of the realm of the mind.

The Inner Flower

For this exercise you will need a flower. With your eyes half closed and half open, look at the entire flower for a few seconds. While you are concentrating, try to feel that you yourself are this flower. At the same time, try to feel that this flower is growing in the inmost recesses of your heart. Feel that you are the flower and you are growing inside your heart.

Then, gradually try to concentrate on one particular petal of the flower. Feel that this petal which you have selected is the seed-form of your reality-existence.

After a few minutes, concentrate on the entire flower again, and feel that it is the Universal Reality. In this way go back and forth, concentrating first on the petal – the seed-form of your reality – and then on the entire flower – the Universal Reality. While you are doing this, please try not to allow any thought to enter into your mind. Try to make your mind absolutely calm, quiet and tranquil.

After some time, please close your eyes and try to see the flower that you have been concentrating on inside your heart. Then, in the same way that you concentrated on the physical flower, kindly concentrate on the flower inside your heart, with your eyes closed.

The Inner Flame

Before you meditate, try to imagine a flame inside your heart. Right now the flame may be tiny and flickering; it may not be a powerful flame. But one day it will definitely become most powerful and most illumining. Try to imagine that this flame is illumining your mind. In the beginning you may not be able to concentrate according to your satisfaction because the mind is not focused. The mind is constantly thinking of many things. It has become a victim of many uncomely thoughts. The mind does not have proper illumination, so imagine a beautiful flame inside your heart, illumining you. Bring that illumining flame inside your mind. Then you will gradually see a streak of light inside your mind. When your mind starts getting illumined, it will be very, very easy to concentrate for a long time, and also to concentrate more deeply.

Concentration on Essential Qualities

In silence kindly repeat the word 'simplicity' inside your mind seven times and concentrate on the crown of your head. Then repeat the word 'sincerity' seven times silently and soulfully inside your heart, and concentrate on your heart. Then kindly repeat the word 'purity'* seven times inside or around your navel centre, and concentrate on the navel centre. Please do all this silently and most soulfully. Then focus your attention on the third eye, which is between and slightly above

---

* *'Purity' refers to the absence of negative thoughts and emotions, doubt, jealousy etc. (See appendix)*

the eyebrows, and silently repeat 'surety' seven times. Next, place your hand on top of your head and say three times, 'I am simple, I am simple, I am simple.' Then place your hand on your heart and say three times, 'I am sincere, I am sincere, I am sincere.' Then place your hand on the navel centre, repeating 'I am pure,' and on the third eye, repeating 'I am sure.'

Meditation Exercises

The Vastness of the Sky

When you want to meditate, at that time think of something very vast – the sky, the ocean, the mountains – and become one with the vastness, which is all power.

Keep your eyes half open and imagine the vast sky. In the beginning try to feel that the sky is in front of you; later try to feel that you are as vast as the sky, or that you are the vast sky itself. After a few minutes, please close your eyes and try to see and feel the sky inside your heart. Please feel that you are the universal Heart, and that inside you is the sky that you meditated upon and identified yourself with. The universal Heart is infinitely vaster than the sky, so you can easily house the sky within yourself.

Nature Meditation

The best way to appreciate nature's beauty is to sit and meditate with nature. If you take a tree as nature, then sit at the foot of a tree and meditate. If you take the sun as an expression of nature, then look at the sun and meditate. If you feel the ocean or sea as nature, then sit in front of the water and meditate. While looking at the tree or the sun or the ocean, try to feel your oneness with it. Anything that you consider as nature or nature's beauty, you should try to become one with. Again, if you want a particular thing from nature, you have to go to that thing. If you want to have vastness, then just go out of the house and look at the sky and you will enter into vastness. If you want to have a very vast, pure consciousness, then stand in front of a river and meditate on the river. And if you want to get height in your life, then go to a mountain and meditate there. So whatever you want, you have to stand in front of that particular thing and invoke it. You have to invoke the spirit of nature or become one with the soul of nature. That is the best kind of identification.

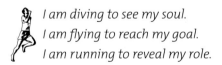

I am diving to see my soul.
I am flying to reach my goal.
I am running to reveal my role.

Feel that You Are a Child

When you start meditating, always try to feel that you are a child. When one is a child, one's mind is not developed. At the age of twelve or thirteen, the mind starts functioning on an intellectual level. But before that, a child is all heart. A child feels that he does not know anything. He does not have any preconceived ideas about meditation and the spiritual life. He wants to learn everything fresh.

First feel that you are a child, and then try to feel that you are standing in a flower garden. This flower garden is your heart. A child can play in a garden for hours. He goes from this flower to that flower, but he does not leave the garden, because he gets joy from the beauty and fragrance of each flower. Feel that inside you is a garden, and you can stay in it for as long as you want. In this way you can learn to meditate in the heart.

If you can remain in the heart, you will begin to feel an inner cry. This inner cry, which is aspiration, is the secret of meditation. When an adult person cries, his cry is usually not sincere. But when a child cries, even if he is crying only for candy, he is very sincere. At that time, candy is the whole world for him. If you give him a hundred-dollar bill, he will not be satisfied; he cares only for candy. When a child cries, immediately his father or mother comes to him. If you can cry from deep within for peace, light and truth, and if this is the only thing that will satisfy you, then God your eternal Father and eternal Mother is bound to come and help you.

I Am the Soul

In order to purify your mind, the best thing to do is to feel every day for a few minutes during your meditation that you have no mind. Say to yourself, "I have no mind, I have no mind. What I have is the heart." Then after some time feel, "I do not have a heart. What I have is the soul." When you say, "I have the soul," at that time you will be flooded with purity. But again you have to go deeper and farther by saying not only, "I have the soul," but also "I am the soul." At that time, imagine the most beautiful child you have ever seen, and feel that your soul is infinitely more beautiful than that child.

The moment you can say and feel, "I am the soul," and meditate on this truth, your soul's infinite purity will enter into your heart. Then, from the heart, the infinite purity will enter into your mind. When you can truly feel that you are only the soul, the soul will purify your mind.

Light and Purity from the Soul

Purity is the light of our soul expressing its divinity through the body, the vital and the mind. When we are pure we gain everything. If we can retain our purity, we will never lose anything worth keeping. Today we may have great thoughts or great inner power, but tomorrow we are bound to lose them if we are not pure. Purity is the Breath of the Supreme. When purity leaves us, the Breath of the Supreme also leaves. Then we are left with only our human breath.

Purity means following the dictates of our Inner Pilot without allowing undivine forces to enter into us. The more we develop divine purity, the greater becomes our inner strength.

Doubt, insincerity, fear, anxiety, jealousy, attachment and all other imperfections or limitations are impurities. Impurity includes insincerity, doubt and all other negative ways of thinking and it is bound to affect both our outer behaviour and our inner progress. Impurity comes from the limited mind, whereas purity comes from vastness. The human mind is impure because the human mind is unable to become one with the Universal Reality. If something is vaster than the vastest – the sky or the sun or the Himalayas – then that vastness itself can give you purity.

There are many keys to open the door of purity, but there is one key which is most effective, and that key is the absence of thought-waves in the mind. When the mind is calm and quiet, purity automatically dawns in the entire being. We can think of the mind as a dark room, a room that has not seen light for many, many years. We need someone who can bring light into this room. That person is the soul. We have to become the most

THE SOUL BIRD

O world-ignorance,
*   Although*
You have shackled my feet,
*   I am free.*

Although
You have chained my hands,
*   I am free.*

Although
You have enslaved my body,
*   I am free.*

I am free because
*   I am not of the body.*
I am free because I am not the body.
I am free because I am the soul-bird
*   That flies in Infinity-Sky.*
I am the soul-child that dreams
On the Lap of the immortal
*   King Supreme.*

intimate friend of our soul, who has the capacity to help us and the willingness to illumine anything that is dark within us. We have to consciously feel that we need the soul just as we need the body. If our need is sincere, then the soul will come forward and illumine our minds.

 Paradise is not a place;
It is a state of consciousness.

The Power of a Mantra

Mantra is a Sanskrit word. In Indian philosophy, spirituality and the inner life, mantras play a considerable role. A mantra is a syllable divinely surcharged with power.

If you cannot enter into your deepest meditation because your mind is restless, this is an opportunity to utilise a mantra. You can repeat 'Supreme' or 'AUM' or 'God' for a few minutes.

Chanting a mantra can be done while you are driving or walking along the street or standing in a public place. If you silently chant while walking along the street, you are not withdrawing; only you are trying to protect yourself from the unaspiring world. You are increasing your inner strength and inner capacity. Then, when you are inwardly strong, you will no longer have to chant; you can just move around and not be disturbed.

Aum is a single, indivisible sound; it is the vibration of the Supreme. Aum is the seed-sound of the universe, for with this sound God set into motion the first vibration of His creation. The most powerful of all mantras is Aum; Aum is the mother of all mantras. At every second God is creating Himself anew inside Aum. Without birth is Aum, without death is Aum. Nothing else but Aum existed, exists and will forever exist.

The sound of Aum is unique. Generally we hear a sound when two things are struck together. But Aum needs no such action. It is *anahata*, or unstruck; it is the soundless sound. A Yogi or spiritual Master can hear Aum self-generated in the inmost recesses of his heart.

There are many ways to chant Aum. When you chant it loudly, you feel the omnipotence of the Supreme. When you chant it softly, you feel the delight of the Supreme. When you chant it silently, you feel the peace of the Supreme.

It is best to chant Aum out loud, so its sound can vibrate even in your physical ears and permeate your entire body. This will convince your outer mind and give you a greater sense of joy and achievement. When chanting out loud, the 'M' sound should last at least three times as long as the 'AU' sound.

→

Early years. *Photo of Sri Chinmoy taken around 1947 at the Sri Aurobindo Ashram in Pondicherry, South India.*

CHAPTER FOUR

The Life
of Sri Chinmoy

 *The fulness of life
lies in dreaming
and manifesting the
impossible dreams.*

The Art of Meditation
and its Creative Expression

*Sri Chinmoy was one of very few spiritual masters who combined their highest
inner meditation with remarkable outer expression. In this chapter you will learn
how Sri Chinmoy expressed his inner experiences of meditation in an unprecedented,
creative outpouring of music, art, literary work and continual service to humanity.*

*Sri Chinmoy Kumar Ghose was born in the small village of Shakpura in Chittagong,
East Bengal, India (now Bangladesh) on 27 August 1931 to Yogamaya and Shashi
Kumar Ghose. He was the youngest of seven children. His father, Shashi Kumar, worked
as the chief inspector of the Assam-Bengal Railway for a number of years and later
founded a small bank in Chittagong. Following the loss of his parents, the young
Chinmoy was taken by his elder brothers and sisters to live at a spiritual community*

in Pondicherry, South India. This community – the Sri Aurobindo Ashram – offered a lifestyle centred around Integral Yoga. This well-rounded approach to yoga included daily work in the Ashram 'cottage industries' and the practice of Western sports such as track and field athletics, volleyball and football in addition to the more typically eastern disciplines of meditation, devotional music and composition of spiritual poetry. Sport was seen as an essential ingredient to this holistic lifestyle, facilitating the optimum health required for a dynamic spiritual life.

Chinmoy spent many hours a day on the sports field and developed into a champion athlete, winning the Ashram decathlon event in 1958 and 1959. He also won the 100-metre dash in the Ashram's annual competitions for 16 consecutive years, from 1945 to 1960. Chinmoy also became captain of the men's football and volleyball teams, as well as head coach of both the men's and women's volleyball teams. In addition to this, he cycled for up to two hours a day while carrying out various errands for the General Secretary of the Ashram.

•••

At the end of the day, Chinmoy was naturally exhausted from his sporting practices. Soon after he arrived at the Ashram, however, something most unusual began to happen. At the time, he shared a room with his elder brother Chitta. One night, Chinmoy went to bed as usual, drawing the mosquito net around him. In the middle of the night, he was awakened by the sensation of somebody pinching him. It was Sri Aurobindo who had appeared in a subtle form. "Get up and meditate, Chinmoy!" he said. Chinmoy looked at the clock on the wall. It was only seven minutes past two and he was still extremely tired. He obeyed the Master and sat up in bed to meditate. Inwardly he felt and saw that Sri Aurobindo was instructing him, and he was able to continue successfully with his practice for a number of hours. These nightly episodes continued until Chinmoy had developed the ability to meditate for up to eight hours per day of his own accord, having many profound inner experiences and in subsequent years reaching the highest states of consciousness.

Running barefoot on the Ashram's cinder track.
Sri Chinmoy's personal bests: 100 m – 11.7 s, 400 m – 53.6 s

Beyond the realm of thoughts. *Sri Chinmoy in a rare state of consciousness known as 'nirvikalpa samadhi', where one perceives fully his inseparable oneness with the entire universe.*

At the age of fourteen Chinmoy recorded the following experience which has guided his life.

.•..

Whenever I had the opportunity, I flew to the edge of the ever-blue sea and took my seat there in solitude. My bird of consciousness, dancing slowly, rose to the sky and lost itself up there.

On this occasion – it was a full-moon night – as I gazed and gazed upon the blue-white horizon, I found only light, a sea of sweet and serene light. All was engulfed, as it were, in an infinite Ocean of Light which played lovingly on the sweet ripples.

My finite consciousness was in quest of the Infinite and Immortal. I drank deeply of Ambrosia and was floating on an illumined ocean. It seemed that I no longer existed on this earth.

All of a sudden – I do not know why or how – something put an end to my sweet dream. No longer did the air emit its honey-like immortal bliss, for my own depressed thoughts had come to the fore: "Useless, everything is useless. There is no hope of creating a divine world here on earth. It is only a childish dream." I felt, too, that I could not go on even with my own life. This seemed to be nothing but a thorny desert strewn with endless difficulties.

"Why should I suffer these unbearable pains and sorrows here? I am the son of the Infinite. I must have freedom. I must have the ecstasy of Paradise. This ecstasy resides ever within me. Why then should I not leave this mortal world for my Eternal Abode in Heaven?"

A sudden flash of lightning appeared over my head. Looking up with awe and bewilderment, I found above me my Beloved, the King of the Universe, looking at me. His radiant Face was overcast with sorrow.

"Father," I asked, approaching Him, "what makes Thy Face so sad?"

"How can I be happy, My son, if you do not wish to be My companion and help Me in My Mission? I have, concealed in the world, millions of sweet plans which I shall unravel. If My children do not help Me in My Play, how can I have My Divine Manifestation here on earth?"

Profoundly moved, I bowed and promised: "Father, I will be Thy faithful companion, loving and sincere, throughout Eternity. Shape me and make me worthy of my part in Thy Cosmic Play and Thy Divine Mission."

•●•

It was at the Ashram that Chinmoy also began writing poetry to express his developing mystical vision. By 1957, following a number of different day jobs – including electrician, paper maker and kitchen assistant – his obvious and deeply spiritual literary insight led him to the job of secretary to the poet and savant, Nolini Kanta Gupta. Nolini was the General Secretary of the Sri Aurobindo Ashram. Chinmoy continued in this position until he departed India.

Heeding an inner command, Chinmoy went to America in 1964 with an aspiration to be of service to spiritual seekers in the Western world. He initially worked at the Indian Consulate in New York City and began giving talks and lectures on Hinduism and Eastern spirituality in his spare time. Soon, students became eager to study his spiritual philosophy in more depth and he began his work in earnest as a meditation master, becoming known as Sri Chinmoy.

During the 43 years that he lived in the West, he opened meditation centres in 60 countries and served as spiritual guide to more than 7,000 students. He encouraged a balanced lifestyle, incorporating the inner disciplines of prayer and meditation with participation in the outer activities of contemporary life. A special emphasis was always placed on developing the qualities of the spiritual heart as a method of harmonising the inner and outer aspects of life.

Our path is the path of the heart.
Ours is not a religion – far from it. Ours is only a way of life.

Peace begins with each of us. *The Sri Chinmoy Oneness-Home Peace Run,*
also known as The World Harmony Run.

Sri Chinmoy's boundless creativity found expression not only in poetry and other
forms of literature, but also in musical composition and performance, in art and sport.
Sri Chinmoy offered lectures on diverse spiritual subjects at universities throughout the
world, including multiple visits to Oxford, Cambridge, Harvard, Yale and many other
notable scholastic institutions. He untiringly dedicated his life to the pursuit of friend-
ship, harmony, and greater understanding amongst different peoples and nations.

In 1987 Sri Chinmoy founded the 'Oneness-Home Peace Run', also known as the
'World Harmony Run' – a global torch relay seeking to strengthen international friend-
ship and understanding.

Sri Chinmoy established the 'Oneness-Heart-Tears and Smiles' humanitarian
organisation in the 1990s to serve less fortunate members of the world family by sup-
plying food, medical and educational equipment and other urgent support.

In 1970, at the invitation of U Thant, the third Secretary-General of the United Nations, Sri Chinmoy began twice-weekly lunchtime peace meditations for delegates and staff members. Held at United Nations headquarters in New York, these meditations have continued to this day.

•••

Sri Chinmoy considered music as the universal language of the heart, dissolving barriers of race, language and culture. He composed more than 21,000 songs in his native Bengali and in English.

"It is through music that the universal feeling of oneness can be achieved in the twinkling of an eye," *he says.*

"Meditation and music cannot be separated. Next to meditation is music. But it has to be soulful music, the music that stirs and elevates our aspiring consciousness. If one can play soulful music or hear soulful music, the power of his own meditation increases."

In 1984 Sri Chinmoy offered his first Peace Concert in Cologne, Germany, to an audience of 8,500 people. He then went on to offer in total a monumental 750 Peace Concerts around the world during the remaining years of his life.

> Sri Chinmoy is a miraculous model of the abundance in the creative life, and I can only hope that someday I may participate in that cosmic fountain of stillness and profound energy which he inhabits."
>
> **—Maestro Leonard Bernstein**

In over 1,600 books of poetry, essays, plays, short stories and answers to questions, Sri Chinmoy's words have conveyed the richness and diversity of the quest for peace and self-discovery.

Music is next to meditation. *Sri Chinmoy playing his favourite instrument,*
the Indian esraj.

Fountain-Art. *Sri Chinmoy painted over 140,000 paintings*
and drew almost 16,000,000 'soul-birds', symbolising the freedom of the
human soul (right).

Sri Chinmoy calls his artwork 'Jharna-Kala', which is Bengali for 'Fountain-Art',
reflecting his experience of an inner fountain of creativity. He saw his artwork as a
spontaneous expression of deep inner realities. When asked about his artistic process,
he explained how he 'followed a streak of light' when painting. He often created a
drawing in a few seconds or minutes by remaining in a state of spiritual height and not
allowing the spontaneous flow to be in any way inhibited by mental processing.

"Love and serve" *is the inner philosophy of tennis, according to*
Sri Chinmoy.

Masters Games. *Running the 100-metre final in 15.34 s*
at the World Veterans Games in Miyazaki, Japan (1993)

Unusually for a sprinter, in the 1970s and 1980s, Sri Chinmoy became an active long distance runner, completing 241 races in total, which included 22 marathons and 5 ultra-marathons with a personal best in the marathon of 3:55:07.

•••

In addition to Sri Chinmoy's running feats, for many years – particularly during the 1980s and 1990s – Sri Chinmoy also played tennis almost every day, often practising for up to four hours at a time, such was his enthusiasm for the game.

He says, "Playing tennis reminds us of being an instrument. If you accept the inner philosophy of tennis, which is 'love and serve', then you can derive so much benefit. Also, tennis can give us so much joy because we are playing with someone and there are so many different movements of the body. Tennis is an excellent form of recreation. When you are playing tennis, you are getting so much innocent joy. Because of your joy, you are becoming like a child once more, and that happiness itself is helping you to make progress."

•••

Sri Chinmoy also competed in a number of track and field Masters Games and events over the years, including the World Masters Games in Puerto Rico in 1983 and ten years later in 1993, at the World Veterans Games in Miyazaki, Japan. As a masters athlete, he set the following 100 metre personal bests: at age 52 in the World Masters Games in Puerto Rico he ran the 100 metres in 14:48 s; at age 61, he showed that age has no limits by bettering his 100 metre time to 13.67 s.

•••

For several years, Sri Chinmoy and his students pursued cycling as a discipline, training in the early mornings and even participating in an arduous 24-hour bicycle race held in New York's Central Park. Sri Chinmoy himself completed 230 miles during this race in 1978.

•••

In 1985, at the age of 53, Sri Chinmoy was inspired to begin lifting weights – starting with a 40 pound dumbbell – and soon began lifting astounding weights that challenged common perceptions of what was humanly possible in weightlifting.

↑ ↗

Honouring others. *The marathon champion Paula Radcliffe and the legendary Muhammad Ali with his wife, Lonnie, being lifted by Sri Chinmoy in the Lifting Up the World with a Oneness-Heart programme.*

His 'Lifting Up the World with a Oneness-Heart' programme then saw him physically lifting thousands of people across the globe over a number of years in an effort to celebrate the goodness and inspiration that those people had offered to their fellow human beings.

Sharing the inspiration. *Sri Chinmoy meeting with President Mikhail Gorbachev (above) and President Nelson Mandela (below); also present is David Dinkins, Mayor of New York City (bottom right)*

Sri Chinmoy's devotion to the ideal of oneness amongst all of humankind touched the hearts of many world luminaries who enjoyed personal friendships with Sri Chinmoy, including Mother Teresa, Archbishop Desmond Tutu, President Mikhail Gorbachev and President Nelson Mandela.

Your untiring efforts and continuous travels worldwide to spread the message of peace and the oneness of humanity are indeed admirable, my brother, and we offer all our support and encouragement for your peace initiatives."

—President Nelson Mandela

On 11 October, 2007, Sri Chinmoy passed away at his home in Jamaica, Queens, New York. Mikhail Gorbachev commented that his passing was "a loss for the whole world" and that "in our hearts, he will forever remain a man who dedicated his whole life to peace."

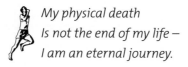

My physical death
Is not the end of my life —
I am an eternal journey.

CHAPTER FIVE

A Mystic Journey In the Weightlifting World

Mine is the heart
To challenge at every moment
My life's limits.

There are countless people on earth who do not believe in the inner power, the inner life. They feel that the outer strength and the outer life are everything. I do not agree with them. There is an inner life; there is spirit, and my ability to lift these heavy weights proves that it can work in matter as well.

In my life running is unparalleled; it has no second. Weightlifting was never my forte. Right from my early years I disliked bodybuilding and weightlifting. I was a sprinter and decathlete, and I did not care for weightlifting at all. It was something foreign to me. But last year [1985] I started weightlifting because of an inner command. If one prays and meditates sincerely, somebody within him talks to him and tells him what to do and what not to do. You use the term 'God'; I say my 'Inner Pilot'. I always listen to the dictates of my Inner Pilot, and my Inner Pilot asked me to enter into weightlifting. That is the main reason, the inner reason, why I took up weightlifting.

Name and fame as such, what most of the world craves for, is not what I want. Only I want the manifestation of God's Will, to show that the spirit can be manifested in and through the body. My goal is not to be a bodybuilder or a weightlifter of the highest magnitude. If what I am doing is considered unprecedented, then it is well and good. But I will not aim at a world record as such. It is not that I will try to break a world record by hook or by crook – far from it! I will try to transcend myself. While transcending myself, it is up to the Will of the Supreme if I will do a little better than others have done. I want to increase my capacities, I want to go beyond and beyond, so that others will be inspired to do the same.

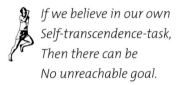

If we believe in our own
Self-transcendence-task,
Then there can be
No unreachable goal.

What I do in lifting heavy weights is something really significant on the physical plane – bringing down light into inconscience. Metal is nothing but inconscience, and to bring down light into matter is a most difficult task. For light to enter into inconscience is a supreme achievement for humanity, because it is inconscience which always fights against light.

On the strength of my prayer and meditation, I have been able to build up my strength and to accomplish something in 15 months which otherwise would have taken me 30 or 40 years to do. Or perhaps I would never have been able to do these things. So my message is that if one needs strength, then uncovering one's inner strength through prayer and meditation is the fastest and most effective way to get it. Inner strength is not my monopoly. Everybody has it. Only it has to be brought forward. Physical strength in comparison to spiritual strength is nothing, absolutely nothing.

Progress with the One-Arm Lift

Sri Chinmoy made astounding progress with his one-arm lift, going from lifting 40 pounds in June 1985 to lifting over 7,000 pounds one year and 7 months later. In the beginning after three months, he had increased his lift by 60 pounds, then added 600 pounds in the following two months. Less than four weeks later he was lifting a remarkable 2,000 pounds, adding another 1,000 pounds within the next two months. Then in a final burst, only ten days later, he moved a 7,000-pound dumbbell with his right arm.

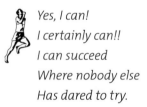 *Yes, I can!*
I certainly can!!
I can succeed
Where nobody else
Has dared to try.

Let us say somebody can lift 60 pounds with only his muscle-power. If the same person prays and meditates for a few minutes before he lifts, then he will have the strength not only of his body but also of his mind and his vital. Now he is getting help only from his physical. He is not getting inner determination from the vital or the tremendous will-power that is inside the mind. He is not even aware of these things. But if he prays and meditates, immediately he feels that his mind has tremendous will-power, tremendous concentration-power. If he thinks of his vital, he sees that it is full of determination. And his body is full of energy. All these good qualities he can feel when he prays and meditates. He feels that his vital, mind, heart and soul are all the friends of his body, and he takes help from them. If somebody has friends, then those friends come to help him when he needs them, and naturally his weightlifting becomes easier.

Continuous self-transcendence. *Sri Chinmoy began by lifting
a 40-pound dumbbell from the ground. Taking help from the
strength within, he quickly increased the weight he was able to lift.*

Overall progression:

40 lbs (26 June 1985)

106¼ lbs (9 Oct 1985)

705¾ lbs (1 Nov 1986)

2,039 lbs (27 Nov 1986)

3,081¾ lbs (20 Jan 1987)

7,063¾ lbs (30 Jan 1987)

I am trying to inspire people who are not praying and meditating. I am telling them that everybody has a vital, everybody has a mind, everybody has a heart, everybody has a soul. But they are not utilising these members of their inner family the way I do. Otherwise, if I had to depend entirely on the physical, I could do next to nothing. I can lift as much as I do because I am taking help from the strength within me. My friends the vital, mind, heart and soul are helping me from within. They are my inner friends. So I am telling those people who are not now aware of the inner life that inner strength is something real. They will be able to increase their capacity tremendously if they also take help from their inner friends.

People see that my physique is nothing in comparison to the physiques of the professional bodybuilders. Their biceps will be 22 inches whereas mine are not even 14, and their calves will be 18 to 20 inches while mine are 13½. Yet I can lift weights that many of them cannot lift. So what does it prove? It proves that the inner spirit, or the mental and psychic power, can be of great assistance to the body when it is brought to the fore. Otherwise my physical body would never be able to lift this kind of weight. It is my prayer-life and meditation-life that, through God's Grace, are enabling me to do this.

I give 100 per cent credit to my prayer-life and meditation-life. In my case, it is not 99½ per cent or 99¾ per cent, but 100 per cent. When I lifted my body-weight with my left arm and then my right arm, I know that if my inner Guide did not protect me, I would have dropped it or I could not have lifted it at all. For everything I do, I depend on His Grace, His Compassion, His Protection.

If God grants us His Compassion, out of His infinite Bounty, then is there anything we cannot do? I am a drop, but the moment I enter into the ocean, I become the ocean. Similarly, my finite will, finite capacity, is next to nothing, but the moment I identify myself with God's infinite Will, I am able to accomplish so much. Otherwise, how could I think of lifting such heavy weights at this age? I would be the first person to doubt it. But again, I know I have not done it, I have not done it. Who has done it? God, my inner Pilot. He is infinite, eternal and immortal. For Him to do this kind of thing is so easy. So for everything, I give Him 100 per cent credit. I know what I can do. I can do nothing. I have written thousands of poems, composed thousands of songs and created thousands of paintings. I know that it is His unconditional Grace at every moment that has enabled me to do these things. I do not deserve it. I know there are many people who are infinitely more talented than I am, but out of His infinite Compassion, He has chosen me.

In the bodybuilding and weightlifting world, look at the biceps and triceps of the champions. How huge they are! But when it comes to lifting, perhaps they are not invoking the highest Power, supreme Power.

●●●

> At the age of 73 he is doing things that I could not do in my prime or even attempted to do back then and I certainly do not attempt to do it now. He drew on a much higher being that helped him accomplish things the average bodybuilder could never do. It is his feats of strength combined with his love that has made such an impact on the world."

—**Bill Pearl** (USA), Five-Time Mr. Universe,
Best-Built Man of the Twentieth Century

I pray and meditate so that I can establish my oneness with each and every human being in the whole world. My lifting is all done on the strength of my heart's oneness with the world. Physical force does not and cannot equal the force of the heart's oneness.

We talk about peace, but talking is not the answer. The embodiment of peace is the answer. The revelation of peace is the answer. The offering of peace to the entire world is the answer. First we have to embody peace, and then we have to reveal and offer peace to the world at large. That is what I am trying to do with my weightlifting.

.•.

On 27 November 1986, Sri Chinmoy succeeded in lifting a 2,039-lb dumbbell. Commenting on the lift, he said the following.

It is through love-power that I did it, not through adamantine will-power. On my face you do see determination-power and will-power when I am lifting. But it is love-power that actually makes it possible for me to lift these weights. Sometimes determination-power can be destructive, but in no way is mine destructive. It is

↑

The strength of love-power. *2,039 lbs (27 November 1986)*

not destruction-power that you are seeing; it is only adamantine will-power on my face, because I have to energise my arm. I have to use a special kind of will-power – electric will-power I call it – on my arm, especially on my wrist. I have many, many types of will-power, but this one is absolutely my strongest and fastest. I keep a very special concentration on my arm, especially my wrist. Ninety percent of the weight is supported by my arm. People will say, "Your shoulder, your back, your legs, and many other muscles are also working." But I know how much my leg muscles are working. Next to nothing! As I am lifting, my whole body is supporting the weight, but in no way are my chest or shoulders or legs actively helping me. My right arm is holding ninety percent of the weight, and my wrist is holding at least seventy-five percent of that. People will laugh, since my wrist is narrower than the narrowest. But I know that at least seventy-five percent of the weight my wrist is holding. So I am always extremely careful with my wrist. All my dynamic energy and will-power are in my right arm and wrist. Otherwise, this tiny wrist would be crushed to pieces.

It is not actually painful, but it is a tremendous task, and very exhausting. Inner strength has to come to the fore, and the physical body has to receive the power that is coming from within. The physical body has to become a pure and perfect instrument of the spirit. I am doing these lifts with the physical body, but the strength and power are coming from within – from an inner source.

•••

I am trying to be of some inner service to people who want to go one step forward. They do not have to lift 2,000 pounds, but perhaps they will take the inspiration that I am offering and make the effort to do something in their own lives which they previously thought was too difficult or impossible. In any field they can get inspiration to do something better than what they have been doing.

Sometimes there is no logic behind my performances. But again, inner inspiration is such that it does not correspond to outer reasoning. Many, many things I have done which my physical mind cannot believe. When I look at the weight, I am frightened to death. But then again, when I concentrate, I am not afraid of it. When I am one with it, I act like a hero. When I am not one with it, when my concentration or my oneness with the weight is not there, then I am actually frightened. But when I try to go beyond the mind, then these barriers do not exist.

Challenging Impossibility

When we live in the heart, there is no such thing as impossibility.

Impossibility is a word that we find in the English dictionary. But this particular word we do not find in our heart's dictionary. Our heart recognises no such word. In our heart we are all the time expanding our own reality and growing from the finite into the Infinite. There what we are dreaming of today is becoming the reality of tomorrow.

There is the reality of the mind and the reality of the heart. When we live in the reality of the mind, we are constantly separating ourselves from others. We sing only one song: my and mine. We know only one truth: division. When we live in the heart, we are constantly expanding on the strength of our oneness with everything around us. There is no division in the heart; there is only multiplication. At every moment we are multiplying our capacities and our inner divinity.

If I ask my mind whether I can lift 7,000 pounds, immediately it will say, "Impossible!" I do not need anyone else in the world to doubt my capacities. My own mind is by far the best doubter. It will do the job better than anybody else. But when I am in the heart, with the heart and for the heart, there is no such thing as impossibility because of the heart's oneness. When I am in the heart, I become one with each and every human being on earth. If countless human beings are with me and for me, then lifting 7,000 pounds is not a difficult task. So through my prayer and meditation I am able to expand my love for my fellow citizens of the world and enter into the Universal Consciousness. For the Universal Consciousness to lift up 7,000 pounds is absolutely nothing. It is like lifting up a grain of sand.

Expanding the reality. *Sri Chinmoy moved this enormous dumbbell 19 months after he started with weightlifting.*

We pray and meditate so that we do not remain in the mind-reality, which is constantly dividing us. We want to remain only in the heart-reality that claims the whole world as its very own. If we remain in the heart and sing the song of universal oneness, we will be able to accomplish everything. The capacity of our heart far transcends the capacity of science. Our prayer-life and meditation-life can take us far, far beyond the domain of scientific capacity.

The word 'impossible' is only in the mind and not in the heart.

↑

With Bill Pearl, *Sri Chinmoy's weightlifting coach and friend (New York, 2007).*

It is humanly impossible for the body's joints to budge this kind of weight. Just to support this kind of weight in any way is a miracle. Sri Chinmoy is not merely lifting a dumbbell. He is trying to lift the attitude of the world. He is showing us that when we reach for the highest through meditation, we can succeed in anything."

—**Bill Pearl**

The very first thing I do before doing heavy lifting is to make my mind absolutely calm and quiet. A mind of complete silence is my secret and sacred key to success and progress. Once we have peace of mind, impossibility cannot exist for us.

Before I lift, I do not think at all because, in general, thinking weakens us. When we are lifting heavy weights, we need the power of concentration. It is like this: let us say I am inside my room and I hear people knocking at the door. I have no idea whether they are my friends or my enemies. So what do I do? I say to myself, "Whatever I have to do inside my room, let me do first. If these people are my real friends, they will wait for me. If they are my enemies, their pride will come forward and they will say, 'It is beneath our dignity to waste our precious time here.' Then they will go away. But my good friends will be sympathetic and say, 'Perhaps he is doing something very important and that is why he is not opening the door.' So they will wait for me indefinitely."

When I am lifting heavy weights, at that time I do not allow any thoughts, whether good or bad, to enter into me. I only pray for God's Grace and then sur-render to His Will. I fold my hands and say, "I would like to become a faithful and devoted instrument of Yours." Human power is so limited; it cannot lift more than a few pounds by itself. It is the divine Power in me, which I have brought to the fore through my prayer-life, that has enabled me to go from 40 pounds to 7,000 pounds.

We have to believe in a higher Power. If we do not believe in a higher Power, then we cannot go beyond our capacity. It is like being in a tug-of-war. When one individual is fighting against another individual, it can be very difficult since each may have the same strength. But if more people come to their rescue and begin pulling with the other contestants, then each team will have greater capacity. Similarly, when I pray and meditate, I feel that somebody else is helping me, whereas an ordinary man feels he can only rely on himself. When he is under the weight, he thinks that he is lifting it all by himself. He has practised for so many years and developed his strength and he feels that everything depends on his physical strength. But in my case, I feel that I am only an instrument. There is some other power that is coming to help me. That power I call God's Grace.

My Lord Supreme,
My Beloved Supreme,
My body's strength
Comes from my mind's happiness.
My mind's happiness
Comes from my heart's gratitude.
My heart's gratitude
Comes from my life's surrender.

I do not give up,
I never give up,
For there is nothing
In this entire world
That is irrevocably
Unchangeable.

Never Give Up!

Every day I am working to achieve my goal. Similarly, in the spiritual life you have to be very regular in order to make progress. How regularly I am trying to lift up heavy weights, but how difficult it is for me! Do not give up. In order to reach your goal, be regular, be determined, be cheerful! Do not give up, do not give up! Continue, continue! The Goal is ahead of you. If you do not give up, you are bound to reach your destined Goal.

The higher the goal, the more patience we need.

•••

In the summer of 1986 Sri Chinmoy experienced a difficult time when he was trying to lift 303 pounds.

I failed 213 times. So many times I failed and failed. But now I am trying to do 320. God knows how many days it will take. What I did yesterday was a personal record. But all the time I am competing with myself. This also is what I teach my students to do. Always compete with yourself; do not compete with anybody else. It is stupidity on our part to compete with others. If I think that I am the best boxer, immediately I will turn around and see a Muhammad Ali there. In any field, if anybody claims to be the best, I tell you, he is a fool, because sooner than at once somebody else will come up out of the blue and defeat him. But if we compete only with ourselves, we will remain not only the present but also the future champion.

Today I have lifted 300 pounds. Tomorrow if I can do 310, then who is defeating me? I am defeating myself. So here there is no defeat; there is only progress, and progress is what we want. Success we cannot depend on, because somebody will always come along and make our success pale into insignificance. When we live in the success-world, sooner than at once we are doomed to frustration. But when we live in the progress-world, always there is tremendous joy. This joy comes not only from transcending one's capacities but from the effort itself. Say I have set my goal at 300 pounds, and I cannot do it. The very fact that I have been devotedly practising and practising gives me joy, and the tenacity or perseverance that I am showing is itself progress. Anything that we do devotedly and soulfully helps us make progress.

So always we have to compete with ourselves in every field. If I have teeming doubts, then I will pray and meditate to minimise and decrease my doubts, and that will be my progress. If I have 10 desires – I want a Cadillac, three houses and so forth – then I will reduce my desires to nine, then eight and like that, finally, to one or no desires. This is how we can have peace of mind. If we have wisdom, we will try to minimise our earthly necessities and increase our heavenly necessities. With our prayer-life and meditation-life we will try to become a better person by minimising our uncomely qualities like jealousy, insecurity and impurity. But if we have an iota of purity or an iota of love, then we will try to increase it. Positive qualities we shall try to increase and negative qualities we shall decrease and diminish.

In order to do that, we have to accept the world and live in the world. Here on earth each of us has to become a good person. If we can become a good person on earth and leave behind us our good qualities, then the whole world will make progress as we go farther and deeper and higher. In this way, each individual has the capacity to offer something for the betterment of the world.

Advice for Weightlifters and Bodybuilders

Concentrate before you lift

Absolute beginners should not meditate at all; they should concentrate. For an absolute beginner, meditation is a difficult process. A beginner has to first learn concentration. When he concentrates, his concentration must be on the tiniest part of the weight that he is trying to lift. Suppose I am trying to lift 200 pounds. On one side of the bar is 100 pounds and on the other side is 100 pounds. When I am concentrating, I will focus my attention on my wrist or on my hand, and try to feel the whole weight there. I will not think of the plates on either side. Everything has to be felt at the spot where I am concentrating. While I am concentrating, I have to feel that the weight is smaller than the smallest – no matter how big it is.

Take deep breaths

It is always good to take deep breaths, not shallow breaths. When I lift very heavy weights, I take three very deep breaths before lifting. The best thing is to feel the breath or the life-energy in your spiritual heart and in your forehead. While you are concentrating, you can feel the same life-energy inside your wrist or inside your palm. It is life-energy that enables us to lift.

Find your invisible friend

The weightlifters and bodybuilders must find an invisible friend who will help them. They must feel that there is Somebody who is eager to help them. They cannot see Him with their eyes, but they can feel Him inside their heart. Many things we cannot see but we can feel.

Let us say that yesterday some young students lifted 200 pounds. They must feel that they have got this capacity from God. If they cannot give credit to God,

Smart Car lift. At the culmination of a public weightlifting exhibition in New York (November 2004), Sri Chinmoy lifted a car weighing the total of 2,229 lbs (1,012 kg) using a standing calf raise machine with a suspended platform beneath.

they should at least give credit to an invisible friend. Or let them say there is a higher force.

They know their own body because they have worked with it for a long time to develop their muscles. But do they also know what their mind can do? When they have a negative thought, they become so weak! Again when they have a positive thought, how strong they become! While they are lifting, if they think of their rivals, they are bound to fail. At that very moment, they should not think at all. But if they have to think, they should think of their coach who is helping and encouraging and inspiring them.

Become one with the weight

The best thing, however, is not to think of anybody, but to become one with the weight itself. If the weight and I have become friends, then we do not need anybody else. But if I cannot take the weight as my friend, at least let me think of my coach – that he is so kind to me and is always trying to help me. And if I cannot think of my coach, then at least let me think of the joy I get from lifting and not of somebody else who perhaps is stronger than I am.

There are so many ways we can improve if our mind is trained to think in a positive or divine way. We have so many friends within us and around us. We have to accept the world as our friend, and not as our enemy.

SRI CHINMOY'S HEAVIEST LIFTS

215,808 lbs Total lifted in one day at his weightlifting exhibition (13 November 2004)

7,063¾ lb Right Arm Dumbbell Lift (30 January 1987)

7,040¼ lb Left Arm Dumbbell Lift (04 August 1988)

2,400 lb Standing Calf Raise (26 September 2004)

1,650 lb Seated Calf Raise (26 September 2004)

1,400 lb Seated Double Dumbbell Overhead Lift (07 May 2005)

1,200 lb (600 lbs + 600 lbs) Double Dumbbell Bench Press (25 July 2005)

↑ ↗

Some of the heavy lifts. *Lifting the 2004 Russian Olympian gold medallist in the long jump, Tatyana Lebedeva, on an elephant using a standing calf raise platform. (Right) Setting his standing calf raise personal record of 2,400 lbs.*

 My Supreme, my Supreme, my Supreme!
When I reach the top,
I cannot stop
And I do not stop
Because I clearly see
A new goal beckoning me.
My Supreme, my Supreme, my Supreme!

CHAPTER SIX

Carl Lewis, the Inner Champion

Sri Chinmoy has shown me that if you just follow the Supreme in yourself and also challenge yourself, then there are really no limits. **—Carl Lewis**

Carl Lewis (USA), born 1 July 1961, became one of the greatest track and field stars of all time. His career spanned from 1979 to 1997 and included 9 Olympic gold medals and one silver. His performance at the 1984 Olympics earned him 4 gold medals in the 100m, 200m, long jump and 4×100m relay – an achievement equalling that of Jesse Owens in the 1936 Olympics.

On 11 November 1983 Carl Lewis met for the first time with Sri Chinmoy, whose advice and practical tips helped him throughout his Olympic career. As Sri Chinmoy became

The inner coach and the outer coach. *Running together in Houston, USA (1992).*

*his inner coach for concentration and meditation, he became the outer coach for
Sri Chinmoy's sprinting. After his Olympic career they maintained a close friendship.*

> My relationship with Sri Chinmoy just started spiritually, because he was so powerful, so loving, positive and uplifting. That was a positive thing that helped me with my club, with my teammates and in my relationships. Later as an athlete he inspired me to continue on. When I saw Sri Chinmoy at his age lifting weights and lifting cars, I felt I had to evolve as a person and as an athlete.
>
> "I have read many things, but one thing that always sticks out in my mind is the way Sri Chinmoy always talks about going forward, going ahead. I have a chance to see that because, as an athlete, I have had wonderful times and difficult times. But as long as we keep focused ahead, we are able to do what we have to do in life."
>
> **—Carl Lewis**

At the start of the 1984 Olympic season Carl Lewis met with Sri Chinmoy to learn more about concentration and meditation.

Carl Lewis: I was mentioning that concentration and meditation have always been foreign to me. I didn't feel I could sit down and meditate and be totally relaxed. What paves the way for the inner life?

Sri Chinmoy: In order to find the inner man, you have to walk along the path of the heart where there is true love, true peace, true light and true delight.

What you now need is meditation. If you didn't have the power of concentration, you could never be the fastest human. You do have it. At every moment I observe in your life the power of concentration. But the power of meditation, which is infinite peace, you have to develop. So if you meditate regularly, then like the power of concentration, without fail you will also get the power of meditation.

Concentration gives us the victory. But meditation gives us joy and confidence. After we have achieved the victory, a kind of fear may enter into our mind that tomorrow perhaps we will not be so fortunate. Today you have won; you are so happy. But a few minutes later you may think, perhaps Calvin Smith will do better in the next meet. Perhaps the day after tomorrow I will not be able to perform as well. Even when concentration brings the victory, you are always afraid that

Practical tips. *At the first meeting of Carl Lewis with Sri Chinmoy in New York (1983).*

Everybody is appreciating,
Admiring and adoring
Your outer achievements.
But you have to know
That this outer glory
Lasts only
For a fleeting moment.

If you make a mistake
In spite of your best intentions,
Remember this mantra:
"The past is dust."

you will not be able to perform well or that somebody else will surpass you. So it is very important to have the power of meditation so that doubt will not be able to attack you and take away your joy. When you win with the power of meditation, you have won for mankind, and that victory will forever last.

Carl Lewis: How should I pray when I am preparing for competition, during the practice time and also right before a race?

Sri Chinmoy: If you can pray to the Supreme with an eagerness to please Him and fulfil Him, then He will run the race in and through you and also for you. Always feel that you are running not for yourself but for Him-only to please Him. If we try to please ourselves in our own way, we will never be satisfied. But when you pray to God to fulfil Himself in and through you, you will be the happiest person no matter what you achieve because God will give you His own Happiness.

When you pray to God before practising and also before a race, feel that you are an instrument. Feel that God Himself, your Beloved Supreme, is running in and through you. Then you will be the happiest person no matter what results come from your sports, because you will get the highest joy by becoming a supremely choice instrument of His.

Now you are happy because you are the fastest runner. You have received just a drop of outer joy, but this drop makes you feel that you are the happiest person. But when you become the fastest runner, the supreme hero, in the inner world, the joy that you receive is infinite. At that time you become the happiest person by becoming one with your own infinite Light and Delight. When this happens, the outer happiness that you previously felt fades into insignificance.

Preparing for the Olympics in 1984

This is part of the message that Sri Chinmoy sent to Carl Lewis on 18 February 1984 at a time when the champion athlete was experiencing some difficulties in his indoor competitions.

While you are running, try to feel that you are being chased rather than being pulled by something or someone. That way you will go faster. If somebody is chasing you, your speed will be faster than if somebody in front of you is pulling you toward him with a rope. If you feel that a magnet is pulling you to the finish line, you will run fast; but you will run faster if you feel that somebody is chasing you and you are running for your life. Imagine that a ferocious tiger is right behind you and at any moment is going to devour you. You know how fast a tiger can run! So you will run for your most precious life, and you will run the fastest.

Getting Confidence for the 1988 Olympics

Sri Chinmoy had the following conversation with Carl Lewis on 3 March 1988.

With the long jump, always feel that you have the capacity to become the Olympic champion. Do not allow yourself even for one second to be intimidated by the thought, "Perhaps I cannot do it." That 'perhaps' has to disappear from your mind totally. In fact, feel that you have already done it. Whenever you try either the 100 metres or the long jump, please feel that you have already done it. With that kind of confidence you will run; with that kind of confidence you will jump. Do not for even one second think of the other runners or jumpers. No, no! You do not have any time to think about them or even to hear about them. It is not that you do not like them. It is just that whenever you think about them or hear about them, very often uncomely or distracting thoughts come. So do not think of others at all. Just feel that you yourself are your own best rival.

I have so much confidence in you. How I wish you would feel the same confidence in yourself when you run and jump, for you have to know that your confidence is your fastest speed; your confidence is your longest jump. And this confidence you will be able to bring to the fore through your prayer-life and your meditation-life. Each time you pray and meditate, just feel that you are transcending yourself. And once you start transcending, then naturally nobody else can come to where you are. You are always at your supreme height.

Every day you spend perhaps two or three hours practising your running and jumping. If every day you can also pray and meditate for just five minutes in the morning and evening and, if possible, at noon also, it will help you immensely. Prayer is your inner strength and your inner power, and this inner power is infinitely stronger than any outer strength.

When I look at the 7,000-pound weight that I lifted, I am the first person not to believe I did it. If I use my mind, I will be my own worst doubter. But I know that it is the Supreme in me who has done it because He wanted to express Himself in and through me in this way. In your case, it is exactly the same. You do not see this because you do not yet have the inner vision to see the invisible. But when we develop the inner vision, we see that although God is infinite, eternal and immortal, He Himself is progressing in and through us. At every moment He is more than eager to help us. Unfortunately, we try to rely all the time on our own capacities. We say, "I can do this, I can do that." But the capacities that we have on the physical plane will not always help us. If we become His instrument and allow Him to manifest Himself in and through us, then He gives us such confidence.

Whenever you come, I offer my oneness in the form of advice, but please feel that my affection and concern for your success are boundless, boundless, boundless. So wherever you are – whether in Texas or Germany or any place – please pray three times a day most soulfully. It is especially important to do this before the Olympics. It is like being a student. The student studies throughout the year, but before the examination he works hard, harder, hardest – more diligently and more soulfully than before.

Carl Lewis: I just wanted to say that this is a really special time and special year for me. I really believe it is a year for me to put to use every tool that I have in order to be the best. I want to do more than just thank you for the motivation you give me and for continually understanding my needs and fulfilling them and giving me energy when I need it.

Sri Chinmoy: The outer life is limited, but the inner life is unlimited; the inner energy that comes from the Source is unlimited. Again, the outer life also can become limitless if it establishes its inseparable oneness with the inner life. You were just speaking about energy. This energy is inexhaustible; it is birthless and deathless. But there is only one way to have access to this energy, and that is through prayer and meditation. There is no other way. To achieve an earthly thing in life there can be several ways. But if it is something really significant, abiding, everlasting – if it is some significant success, progress or glory that you want to offer to God – then you have to bring forward this inner energy. In the inner world it is at our disposal, but most people do not care to bring it forward. Those who do are able to offer something most special both to humanity and to divinity.

I am very, very glad that you have made the inner life part and parcel of your existence. So please, please, every day pray and meditate – just for five minutes in the morning and at night and, if possible, also at noon. So my request to you is: dive deep within, and from your own prayer-life bring forward your limitless energy. Then success will be all yours.

100 Metre Final at the 1988 Olympics

Sri Chinmoy went to Seoul, Korea, to watch Carl Lewis compete during the 1988 Olympics. He met with him in Seoul on 25 September the day after Carl Lewis lost in the 100 metre final. In a dramatic race, Lewis, the defending 100-metre champion, lost to Ben Johnson. As the year before in the world championship final in Rome, Lewis was shocked by Ben's "jumping" start and he looked over three times in disbelief of this enormous starting speed. Johnson won in 9.79 seconds, a new world record, while Lewis ran 9.92. Three days later, Johnson tested positive for drugs, his medal was taken away and Lewis was awarded gold and credited with a new Olympic record.

Sri Chinmoy: Now please tell me, why did you – a world champion – have to glance to the right side after 75 metres? Even a beginner, a novice, would first and foremost be advised not to do that. It is such a deplorable mistake! I was so sad when I saw you looking at him. Originally your goal was in front of you, but then you changed your goal. He became your goal instead of the tape. You have such determination, such will-power, that you easily could have fought him right up to the end. But instead, you did not maintain your adamantine will, and after 75 metres you surrendered. How did it happen?

Carl Lewis: I have no explanation. When I saw he was so far out, I was shocked for the first time. You are right.

Sri Chinmoy: I am telling you, until the very last moment nothing is decided. In boxing there are 12 rounds. Even if someone is leading in points after the 11th round, still you can knock him out in the 12th round. Then he is gone! So if you knock him out, those points are not counted. Similarly, no matter how far you are behind someone else, all that matters is who touches the tape first. The goal is not won until then. Let us say he is winning the first few rounds. But those rounds do not mean anything. If you are determined that in the last round you are going to destroy him, then why do you have to worry about the first few rounds?

I tell you these things to convince your mind. No matter how many metres ahead of you your opponent is, as soon as you look at him, you are entering into his consciousness, and your own consciousness you are losing. You are surprised and shocked that he is ahead of you. But when you are shocked you are invoking a kind of force inside yourself that enters into him and helps him. But if you only think of your goal, then you are entering into God's Consciousness, and God is helping you. It is like this. When you think of your opponent – even if you are thinking of how you will defeat him – a little bit of your determination goes into him and adds to his capacity. But if you think only of your goal, then God comes to increase your determination.

It is easy for me to talk, but I only wish to express my sympathy and remind you that the next time, even if someone is four metres ahead, this person is not your goal. The finish line remains your goal.

The Ground Has a Heart

On 24 June 1989, when Carl Lewis was in Paris for a major track meet, Sri Chinmoy also happened to be in Paris to give a Peace Concert. Carl Lewis recollects a conversation he had with Sri Chinmoy when the spiritual teacher visited him in his hotel.

Carl Lewis: Before today, I thought I had heard all the excuses for running a bad race, failing to meet expectations or just missing a world record. But this morning I was introduced to a new explanation: the ground has a heart, and our relay team had not been in France long enough to feel that heart, to be comfortable with that heart, before our race.

The explanation came from Sri Chinmoy, who was in Paris for another road run to promote world peace. I was glad when I heard Sri Chinmoy was here, because he had wanted to meet my teammates, and this was a good opportunity for that. In our hotel lobby, Joe DeLoach, Floyd Heard, Leroy Burrell and I visited with Sri Chinmoy. He was surprised when he heard we had arrived only a day before the meet.

"This explains why you did not win the world record," said Sri Chinmoy, his words coming slowly, his eyes opening and closing as he spoke, his head nodding gently as he focused on his thoughts. "The ground has a heart. Everything has a heart, a spirit and a heart. When you fly here you have to be on the ground long enough to feel the heart. Yes, that is important. And you missed the record by only a little bit. In a new place – you have to understand this – you have to be on the ground longer before you race."

I smiled and nodded, familiar with the way Sri Chinmoy explains things. But my teammates were a bit stunned. They did not say much to Sri Chinmoy. They just observed.

Sri Chinmoy gave me a birthday cake, a week early, but he wanted me to have it. Sri Chinmoy wished us good luck for the rest of our trip, and that was that.

Back in my room, Joe, Floyd and Leroy agreed on a one-word summary of what they had just seen: "Interesting."

Before going to Tokyo in August 1991 for the World Championships, Carl Lewis said to Sri Chinmoy, "I'm going to take your advice and go two weeks early." At those games Carl Lewis set a new world record of 9.86 for 100 metres at the exceptionally advanced age (for a sprinter) of 30!

Carl offered the victory of this new world record to his father Bill who had passed away one year earlier. After returning to America, Carl Lewis, along with his mother and sister, visited Sri Chinmoy in New York. Sri Chinmoy welcomed them with the following words:

I am so proud of you for offering your victory to your father. Here is the proof that you believe in the spirit. An ordinary human being would say, "Oh, my father is now gone." But you have kept such a strong and powerful inner connection with your father's heart. That means you have kept the connecting link between earth and Heaven.

Your heart is drawing cosmic strength, cosmic energy, cosmic light from Above. You have many inner friends, but they are invisible. I call them divine forces. They are working so powerfully and successfully in and through you. When you are jumping or running, in addition to your physical capacity, so much cosmic energy, cosmic light, cosmic power is coming to help you. These invisible capacities you can see only when you use the inner eye, the third eye. If you use your inner eye, you will see that you have so many friends who are dying to help you. That is because your victory is their victory, just as their victory is your victory. But if you want to rely entirely on earthly help, then this inner help you do not get.

Carl Lewis Coaching Sri Chinmoy

On 1 November 1991 Carl Lewis came to Sri Chinmoy's running track in New York to offer him more coaching tips.

Carl Lewis advises Sri Chinmoy: Once you get up to full speed and your arms are swinging, just let your legs follow your arms. If you keep your arms going the whole time, your legs will follow. *(Sri Chinmoy continues exercising)*

Carl Lewis: You look fine. You're staying relaxed and letting your arms swing. There is only one thing: just make sure your jaw is relaxed. Other than that, your arms and shoulders are swinging and you're turning over.

Sri Chinmoy: Even then, I have my same eternal problem: how to increase my stride.

Carl Lewis: If you stay relaxed and just let your feet turn over, you will just keep the stride but increase the pace so you run faster. Your stride length is fine, but by being relaxed and turning over, you will just go faster and faster. Unlike us, most of the time you remember what you are supposed to do. *(Sri Chinmoy sprints again)*

Carl Lewis: Your legs are more relaxed and you're letting your arms swing. The arms really dictate the stride; you can't have a longer stride than your arms can dictate. So when we got you to swing your arms, that basically told your legs how far to go. A lot of times people try to get a long stride before they deal with their arms, and their stride is longer than their arm swing. Then everything is out of sync. That's why I really focus on the arms because they tell the legs what to do. So just stay relaxed and keep turning over and don't try to reach or stretch at the end. Just keep that stride turning over. That's the way to get your speed. Well, I wish to God the people at University of Houston were so easy to coach. They're all kids and they're tough to teach. Every day you tell them the same thing over and over, but they don't learn anything!

Sri Chinmoy: Then I am a good student?

Carl Lewis: Yes, you're a very good student because you listen and learn.

Sri Chinmoy: I am dying to listen to you. I always set a goal, and then I try to go beyond and beyond. Self-transcendence itself is my goal. So my immediate goal is 13 seconds. By April, I want to run the 100 metres in under 13 seconds. Something within me is telling me that I will be able to do it. Then gradually, gradually I have to come to my dreamland, which is 11.7 seconds. That was my best timing when I was in the Ashram in India. Once I reach 11.7 seconds, then I have to go to 11.6. So, do you think it is possible?

Carl Lewis: Yes, but you have to work.

Sri Chinmoy: I am working.

Carl Lewis: The way you are going to get faster is to just keep working hard at it and wanting to do it. So many people have the capacity to be fast, but they all fall short because they do not want to work at it hard enough. But you also have to make sure that you do not overwork in your running. And if you ever feel tired, take a rest. If you ever feel you are not as excited on a certain day, just take a break – because there is always a reason.

Last number. On August 27th 1997, Carl Lewis, visiting with his mother Evelyn Lewis, offered Sri Chinmoy as a gift the race number of his last race, thanking him for 14 years of advice in concentration and meditation at four Olympic Games.

↗

The champion's spikes. Sri Chinmoy holding in his hands the world record shoes from the 1991 Tokyo World Championships which Carl Lewis gave him as a gift for his 60th birthday.

CHAPTER SEVEN

The Spirit of Running

*To run from the known
To the unknown
Is to run from bondage
To freedom.*

I wish to say that running has its own inner value. While you run, each breath that you take is connected with a higher reality. While you are jogging, if you are in a good consciousness, your breath is being blessed by a higher inner breath. Of course, while you are jogging if you are chatting with one of your friends about mundane things, then this will not apply. But if you are in a good consciousness while you are running, each breath will connect you with a higher, deeper, inner reality.

If you want to get the benefit of a higher force or higher reality for your physical body, then running is absolutely necessary. I am not saying that you have to run the fastest. Even while jogging, you can feel that you have two breaths. One is a higher breath. Something is pulling you up or you are carrying yourself up. The other is your body's breath. The two are combined together.

•●•

Running reminds us of our inner journey, which is ahead of us. The goal is ahead and we are running towards the goal. It is a great feeling, which eventually grows into a great achievement.

Running is continuous motion. Because of our running, we feel that there is a goal – not only an outer goal but also an inner goal. Running helps us by showing us that there is a goal. Again, running itself is a goal for those who want to keep the body in perfect condition.

Running offers us the message of transcendence. In our running, every day we are aiming at a new goal. It is like a child who studies in school. First he studies in kindergarten, then he goes to primary school, then to high school, college and university. After getting his university degree, still he is not satisfied. He wants to achieve more wisdom, more knowledge. Similarly, every day we are running towards a goal, but when we reach that goal, we want to go still farther. Either we want to improve our timing or increase our distance. There is no end. Running means continual transcendence, and that is also the message of our inner life.

Through prayer and meditation, we can develop intense will-power, and this will-power can help us do extremely well in our outer running.

Meditation is stillness, calmness, quietness, while the running consciousness is all dynamism. Again, the runner's outer speed has a special kind of poise or stillness at its very heart. An aeroplane travels very fast, yet inside the plane we feel no movement at all. It is all tranquillity, all peace; and this inner tranquillity we can bring to our outer life. In fact, the outer life, the outer movement, can be successful only when it comes from the inner poise. If there is no poise, then there can be no successful outer movement. Poise is an unseen power, and this unseen power is always ready to come to the aid of the outer runner.

∙●∙

Running for Inner Happiness

Your outer smile can help your running considerably.

Everybody wants to be happy and many people have discovered that running is a very effective way to bring about happiness. This is because running demands not only the fitness of the body but also the fitness of the vital, mind and heart.

We are composed of the body, the vital, the mind, the heart and the soul. These parts are members of the same family. They are supposed to go together. The eldest brother is the soul. Then comes the heart, then the mind, then the vital, then the body.

Sometimes the body is fit enough to run but the mind is not ready. Sometimes the mind wants to run, but the body does not want to cooperate. So we see that all the members of the family – body, vital, mind and heart – have to work together. It is like a family gathering, a family party. The head of the family has invited all the members to come and eat. If one son comes and another does not, the parent cannot be happy. The soul is the head of the family. Through running, it wishes to offer a feast to all its children. Its joy will not be complete if even one member – the body, vital, mind or heart – does not participate. All the children must come to enjoy the feast.

Running keeps the body, vital, mind and heart fit so that the soul can get complete happiness. Today people realise that running can bring the members of the life-family together. They also see that running helps them fight physical ailments and disease. A disease can enter your body as an uninvited guest; before you realise it is your real enemy. But running, by making you healthy, helps you to recognise illness sooner and to keep it from attacking you.

Running is also an excellent way to rid oneself of frustration and anger. If you are really angry with someone, go and run. After a mile or so you will see that your anger has gone away, either because you are totally exhausted or because the satisfaction that you gain from physical exertion has replaced your anger.

Whenever you show aggression or anger, immediately your inner strength goes away. Never think that anger is strength. Anger is absolutely weakness. As soon as you become angry, immediately your psychic strength from your heart goes away. So when the anger-attack comes, you have to say, "I will have nothing to do with you." Try to maintain your inner poise.

A Mantra for Running

While running, if you can repeat the Name of the Supreme most soulfully and devotedly, then naturally it will help you improve your speed and endurance. If you want a mantra, then 'Supreme' is the best mantra. If you want a special type of meditation, then 'Supreme' is the best type of meditation. Just try to repeat the Name of the Supreme most soulfully. It will help you improve your speed and increase your power of endurance.

When you start running, inwardly write down on the top of your head, "No mind, no mind!" Inside the mind is determination, but inside the heart is will-power, psychic will-power. If you can use the will-power that the mind has in the form of determination, good. But it is no match for the heart's psychic will-power.

Should children run long distance?

It is my inner feeling, my spiritual, yogic feeling, that it is not at all good for children to run long-distance; it is not good for their growth. An Indian child should not run more than one mile if he is under thirteen years of age. But for Americans, I would put the age at ten years. Children under ten should not run more than a mile [1.6 km]. If they want to run three miles [about 5 km], they should be at least thirteen years of age. These children will live on earth for many years. Right now let them do sprinting. Let them do 50, 60 or 200 metres; let them do 400 metres or 800 metres maximum. But children's lung capacity and heart condition may not be strong enough for long-distance running – especially children who are in their formative years. Perhaps doctors will say that long-distance running is good for children, but I feel it may lead to some serious problems and is very dangerous. I really feel very sad that parents are not wise in this matter. They are really doing an injustice to their children. A seed germinates, and then it becomes a plant. If you speed up its growth unnaturally, it may grow a little taller. But if you raise it too high, there will be no roots there. It won't be able to grow into a normal, natural tree.

Does bicycle training improve running?

I did a great deal of bicycling when I lived in India in my youth. For at least two and a half hours every day I used to cycle as I did errands. It does not increase running speed at all, but something is better than nothing. Sometimes cycling can actually be a hindrance to running speed, because it develops special kinds of muscles which do not complement the speed muscles. Bicycling does help for endurance, but if you want to increase your running speed, then I do not advise it. You can cycle for endurance, or if you are injured and cannot run. For a little bit of stamina you can do it. But again, cycling stamina is totally different from running stamina. If one wants to become a good runner and maintain a five-minute pace [per mile], then cycling is not the answer. Quality road work is the answer.

Marathon Running

The marathon is a long journey. Of course, there is also the ultramarathon, but the marathon is unique and it will always remain unparalleled among long-distance runs. Just as the marathon is a long journey on the outer plane, so is spirituality a long, longer, longest journey on the inner plane. Your own spiritual run is birthless and deathless; it is endless.

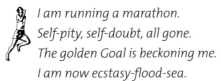

I am running a marathon.
Self-pity, self-doubt, all gone.
The golden Goal is beckoning me.
I am now ecstasy-flood-sea.

↑

The long outer journey *of a marathon reminds us of our long,*
longer, longest inner journey.

When you run a marathon, you are trying to accomplish on the physical plane something most difficult and arduous. When you do this, it gives you joy because it reminds you of what you are trying to accomplish on the inner plane. As you are determined to complete the longest journey on the outer plane, the marathon, so are you determined to reach the Goal in your inner journey. The one journey will always remind you of the other.

Concentration and Meditation for Marathon Running

Before doing sports you can meditate most powerfully to make the mind calm and quiet so that negative thoughts do not enter. Once negative thoughts occupy the mind, they create tension, and this makes you lose all your power of concentration.

It is always advisable to concentrate while running a marathon. If you meditate, then you will feel that you are either on the top of a snow-capped mountain or at the bottom of the sea. That is the very highest type of meditation, but that will not help your running. But if you concentrate on running, then at every moment you will be able to regulate your steps and your forward movement. Also, discouraging, destructive and uncomely thoughts will not be able to lower your consciousness. If your consciousness is not lowered, then naturally you will run faster.

Before running, however, meditation is good to make the mind calm and quiet so that wrong forces do not enter. When you meditate, your mind acquires some poise. Then, while you are running, if you can bring forward this poise, it will help you overcome the mental frustration that often comes while running long distances. When you are running long distances, all kinds of frustrating thoughts will come and make you feel that what you are doing is useless. Or the mind will say, "Oh, this is boring," and you will not want to take one more step. But if you were able to meditate earlier in the day, then you will have acquired some solid inner strength that will carry you mile after mile. Also, meditation teaches you how to empty your mind of thoughts. And if you can keep thoughts out of your mind while you are running, it will help you tremendously – far beyond your imagination. At that time a new creation will be able to dawn inside you, and this will give you added inspiration and receptivity.

Advice to the Sri Chinmoy Marathon Team before the New York City Marathon 1986

Before the race starts meditate for ten minutes. The race starts at 10:45. You do not have to meditate exactly ten minutes before the start, but do not meditate before 10 o'clock. Then after each mile – no matter how badly you are running – for two minutes while you are running the next mile you will offer your

Marathon, marathon, marathon,
Eternity's dawn!
O kindling, streaming flames
Of great Olympic Games,
O Greece-world vision-height,
Cosmos-oneness-delight!
Humanity's transcendence-race,
Divinity's supreme Grace.

gratitude to your Beloved Supreme. Finally, after completing the marathon, even if you are exhausted, dead, also meditate for five minutes and offer your gratitude to your Beloved Supreme. Even if you were trying to run under 2:30 and it has taken you three and a half or four hours, please offer gratitude that you have participated and have run the race cheerfully. Even if you failed miserably to do the time you wanted, your cheerful gratitude will be as good, according to me, as running under 2:30 or whatever your outer goal was.

If you are tired, exhausted, dead, or if you get an injury or cramps, just stop. But if you have to stop, do not feel miserable. Only offer your gratitude. If at the end of 11 miles you have given up, still you have to meditate for five minutes.

How to Run a Faster Marathon

Definitely you will improve your marathon time if you run 10,000 metres on the track. Running is a physical subject, a mental subject, a philosophical subject and a subject of the Beyond. In the mental aspect, if you become used to running shorter distances, it can really help you.

When you are running a marathon, mentally try to feel that you are running only thirteen miles rather than twenty-six miles. If you can convince the mind of this fact, and if the mind can convince the body that it is running only thirteen miles and not twenty-six miles, then it will be a great advantage for you. This is not a mental hallucination. A new discovery has dawned in the mind and the mind is passing it along to the body. Both the mind and the body will have to act together in order to reach the ultimate goal.

Finally, if you can think that through your running you are doing something that has a direct connection with the ever-transcending Beyond, which is far beyond the domain of the earth-bound physical mind, then you will get tremendous inspiration. This inspiration embodies added strength, added joy and an added sense of satisfaction. If you can consciously think of another world – which we call 'the Beyond' – if you can add another vista or dimension to your running, then you are bound to be more successful.

Running Under Two Hours in the Marathon

How I wish the twenty-first century to prove my prophecy that someone will run a marathon in under two hours! I find it very difficult to believe that our human capacity is limited. Right now [1999] the world record for the marathon is 2:06. Just six minutes to reduce over twenty-six miles! Unfortunately, human beings always think, "My capacity, my capacity." If the same world-class runners could say, "My capacity is coming from God. God is running in and through me," and really mean it, then you would see surprising results. There are at least twenty world-class marathon runners. If they could have that kind of faith, you would hear in one month that the world record has been smashed.

Unfortunately, athletes are not all seekers of the highest height. Otherwise, there is not a single record in the athletic world that cannot be smashed mercilessly – even the 100-metre sprint. To me the present record for 100 metres is no record. They can easily bring it down to seven seconds. But who will believe me? Today I am a talker, but one day from Heaven, I will see that my prophecies have come true.

Everything is based on receptivity. In the weightlifting world, if I have to use my physical capacity without depending on God's unconditional Compassion and Grace, do you think I will be able to lift more than fifty pounds with one hand? I doubt it very much. Whether you believe me or say I am exaggerating my self-importance, I want to tell you that a maximum of sixty pounds I would be able to lift with each arm simultaneously. I am able to lift more only because I entirely depend on God's Grace.

Of course, world champions are not seekers of the highest height. But even if they can raise their standard a little, they will achieve so much. Unfortunately, when some world champions perform something extraordinary, outwardly they may fold their hands or they may fall to the ground and look at the sky, but do they really mean it?

When our receptivity increases, God increases our capacity. Before that, all the limitations of the body come and stay indefinitely because of our ingratitude-mind, ingratitude-heart and ingratitude-life. We have to feel that our capacity is coming from God. God has given each of us certain capacities. I may not be a runner, but somebody else may be a runner. I may be a singer, but somebody else may not be a singer. If anyone wants to increase his capacity in his own field, then he must have God-reliance, not self-reliance. Only then will his capacity become unlimited. Now our capacity is limited because we feel we are doing every-thing – we are taking this exercise and that exercise. We give ninety-nine per cent of the credit to what our mind is telling us and our life is prompting us to do. But if we can give one hundred per cent of the credit to God for whatever we are doing that is good and positive in our life, then our capacities will become unlimited.

During a talk Sri Chinmoy mentioned that there are four qualities needed to run the marathon under two hours: Gratitude to Mother Earth in the heart, peace in the mind, purity in the vital and alertness in the body.

Advice to Marathon Champion Paul Tergat

Sri Chinmoy met with Kenyan marathon champion Paul Tergat four days before he won the 2005 New York City Marathon. Sri Chinmoy shared with Paul Tergat his prediction that soon someone would run the marathon in under two hours, and his hope that Tergat would be the first. He then offered him the following advice.

You will have to forget that you are running. Paul Tergat is not running. Somebody else in the Name of God is running in and through you. In that way, your four minutes will disappear and you will be able to run under 2 hours. There is nothing impossible if you try. The 'impossibility' word is found only in the dictionary, but not in the heart, not in the fulfilment of our dreams. The dictionary says 'impossible'. It is the mind. From the brain the word came into existence. When we enter into the heart, the story completely changes.

The tough race. *Paul Tergat outracing Hendrick Ramaala to the finish line of the 2005 New York City Marathon. (Photo © Reuters)*

There is no such thing as impossibility. If our adamantine will comes from within that we are going to do something, nobody can prevent it. Do not use the mind. A child does not use the mind. He just runs and runs and runs. He never becomes tired. If you can feel you are that little child at the age of five or six or seven years old, that unlimited energy again will be bestowed upon you, specially during the last mile. Please at that time surrender to God's Will, and you be the observer. You observe who is running so fast, and you admire that person. Today's dream is tomorrow's reality. Now you are dreaming of something, and tomorrow it will turn into reality.

> Sri Chinmoy was so right in what he told me before the New York City Marathon, that I should keep the focus in the last mile. It was definitely the toughest race in my life. Until the very end we didn't know who would win the Marathon.
>
> "I believe there is a purpose behind the power I got for my athletic life: that I use the sport with the right attitude and for the benefit of my inner life. It is from this power that I have been able to continue until now. Without this higher power I could have easily said: 'Yes, I have broken world records, I have been running well' and I would have left running five years ago.
>
> "Records are set to be broken. I also took the record from somebody else. That means my record does not have to stay forever. It has to be broken. So the sport is really coming out for the development of the world."
>
> **—Paul Tergat**

Paul Tergat won 13 gold medals in World Cross Country Championships. In his long career he broke 6 world records and held the world record for the marathon (2:04:55) from 2003-2007.

Ultra Running

There is no limit to the distance because there is no limit to human capacity. Human capacity depends on our inner hunger – how sincerely we need something or are crying for something.

We are all truly unlimited, if we only dare to try and have faith.

Long distance races remind me of our Eternity's race. Athletes derive tremendous benefits from these multi-day races. They go beyond their capacities. In order to be happy, we have to go always beyond and beyond and beyond our capacities. So here, while running, each runner is getting a very special opportunity to go beyond his or her capacities. Self-transcendence is the only thing a human being needs in order to be truly happy. So these races help the runners tremendously, although outwardly they go through such hardship. Eventually, when the race is over, they feel they have accomplished something most significant.

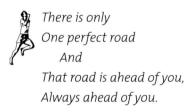

There is only
One perfect road
*   And*
That road is ahead of you,
Always ahead of you.

In the outer world, whether it is a long-distance run or a short-distance run, or jumping or throwing, any extraordinary activity we perform on earth is an indication of the fact that in the inner world that capacity does exist. It is only that we have to use it. The capacity that we appreciate, admire and adore can be seen, felt and acquired in the inner world in infinitely greater measure.

The inspiration that we give to ourselves or to the world by exercising our extraordinary capacity comes from the ever-mounting aspiration of the inner world. Our achievements are for the manifestation of divinity, to add to the receptivity of the outer world, to make the outer world eventually ready to accept the inner capacities of love, peace and bliss in infinite measure.

Always take one more step
Than you intended to.
You can, without fail, do it.
Lo, you have done it.

How can we keep going in a seven day race?

Please do not think of all seven days while you are running. Think of only one day at a time. Then, do not even think of one day; think of only seven hours. Then, for a few minutes, think of only one hour. If you can mentally divide the race and break it down into separate parts, you will get much more energy and much more joy while running. Every time your mind decreases the amount of time you have to run, you will get tremendous inner strength and vigour. So do not keep in mind seven days. Go at your own pace, but mentally divide the race to make the distance as short as possible. In this way, you will always have inner strength and be able to run throughout.

The queen of the frightening distance. *Suprabha Beckjord finishing the 3100-Mile Race in New York, 2007*

The Self-Transcendence 3100-Mile Race

Without courage, life is a path without progress.

Every summer, about a dozen of brave athletes compete in the Sri Chinmoy 3100-Mile Race, held on a half-mile course around a city block in Queens, New York. This is the longest certified footrace in the world; runners must average more than 60 miles per day to finish within the 52-day limit, an amazing challenge. Participants, who include members of the Sri Chinmoy Marathon Team and other ultra runners from all over the world, need tremendous courage, physical stamina, concentration and the capacity to endure fatigue and minor injuries.

Suprabha Beckjord, one of the most enduring ultramarathon runners in the world, has finished the 3100-Mile Race 13 times. Earlier in her career she won the Sri Chinmoy Seven-Day Race five times and held the world record for 1,000 miles as well. To assist Suprabha's intense inner focus, Sri Chinmoy advised her on which qualities to invoke during the 3100-Mile Race in 2000.

There is no 'inwardly' and 'outwardly'. If we feel that there is any difference between the inner life and outer life, then we shall always be failures. There should be no difference between the inner life and outer life – not even an iota.

The question is, what qualities do you need to bring forward from your inner life while you are running? The first one is enthusiasm. Who embodies enthusiasm? A little child. Who can be more enthusiastic than a child? He enters into a garden and runs here and there, here and there, appreciating everything that he sees. Then, in addition to enthusiasm, you need eagerness. Again, who has more eagerness than a little child? If he plays with a toy, he is so eager, his whole world is the toy.

Now, while running 3,100 miles, you have to deal with fatigue – when you are tired, exhausted, dead. As long as you are in the mind, you will always have fatigue, tiredness, weariness and everything. But the moment you enter into the heart, there is no fatigue. What you will find is constant energy.

If you are in the heart, there is a constant supply of energy and sweetness. We all have to develop sweetness. Sweetness is not masculine or feminine. People say that only girls can have sweetness and not men, but sweetness is not something masculine or feminine. Sweetness is a reality which is constantly supplying us with newness and freshness.

While you are running this long distance, you are seeing hundreds of cars passing by and so many people are making noise. But you should feel that you are not running around that big block; you are only running inside your own heart-garden where there are beautiful flowers, plants and trees. If you can not only see but feel that each time you are going around you are only running inside your beautiful heart-garden, then you can bring sweetness into each and every step that you take.

The surface that you run on is solid concrete. When you are running around, after an hour or two hours or a few days, this solid thing that you feel you are striking against starts striking your mind. You start thinking, "This is so bad. Every day I have to do sixty miles," this and that. But who counts the mileage? It is the mind. The mind is saying, "O my God, today I have to do sixty miles, and I have not yet done twenty miles!" Then you are finished! The mind, your worst enemy, is coming to torture you.

But the heart is not counting the mileage. The heart is only running, running, running. Then at the end of that session, the heart says, "Now let me see how many miles I have done." By that time, perhaps you have done forty miles already. The heart does not calculate. The mind calculates from one to two, two to three, three to four and so on. The mind tries to go to the destination by cutting, cutting, cutting. But the heart tries to see and feel the starting point and the end at the same time. For the heart the destination is not somewhere else. Only for the mind is the destination somewhere else. Inside the heart the starting point and the finish line are together. If you can feel that you are a five-year-old or six-year-old child, tiredness will not come into your mind. A child does not know what tiredness is. He knows only enthusiasm and eagerness. Never think of sixty miles or 3,100 miles. Never take the distance in that way – never! Only run for the joy of it.

When you think of the long distance, try to imagine that it is something to play with. Do not think of distance as something you will cover. Do not think that you will be tired, you will be exhausted or you will die. You have to take running as a game you like to play. Any game that you like, feel that you are playing that game. Do not feel that you are running such a long distance, and that every day you are getting tired. No! With tiredness comes sadness, and then you become upset – everything!

Each day when you go out to run, you should see newness, newness, newness. Always think of the heart-garden. When you walk or run in a garden, you do not become tired because of the beautiful flowers and fragrance. Everything is charming, everything is inspiring. When you think of the street, there are only roaring lions here and there, with deafening noise. But while you are running in your own heart-garden, such a sweet feeling you are getting. It is your own garden; you are the boss.

When your mind is operating very powerfully, you are not the boss. Your boss is self-doubt, self-criticism, fear, worry and anxiety. You are constantly thinking, "Will I be able to complete the race?" Those wrong forces become your boss. But when you run inside your heart, then there will be no problem. Always take it as a garden, not as a street, not as a big block.

Do not run with the mind. When you run, if you can make yourself feel that inside your heart Somebody is running or your heart is running or you are running with your heart, then tiredness disappears, the power of distance disappears. Only the power of oneness, oneness, oneness with God's Will appears.

Run,
You can easily
Challenge
The pride of
Frightening distance.

CHAPTER EIGHT

New Insights for Your Training

Your cheerful gratitude will strengthen your body far beyond your imagination.

If one is a seeker-athlete, then before he runs or jumps, before he enters into physical activities, he should offer a few moments of gratitude to his Inner Pilot for inspiring him to become an athlete. An athlete is he who runs, who values time, who values speed and who believes in a goal that ever moves forward. There are millions and billions of people on earth who are not athletes, but he already is an athlete. So if he can offer his gratitude for that, then he increases his receptivity-power. If he increases his receptivity-power, then he automatically increases his athletic capacity. For it is receptivity that increases capacity. The moment he increases his receptivity, he is blessed with more capacity, abundant capacity, boundless capacity. And to increase his receptivity there is only one way: to offer his gratitude-heart for what he has already become. Gratitude means self-offering to one's highest self. Your gratitude is not going to somebody else; it is going to your own highest self. Gratitude helps you identify and feel your oneness with your own highest reality.

Do Your Sport With All Your Heart

With time, I have come to understand that while you are physically strong, you can do thousands of jumps and they all may be technically perfect. However, if you have not put soul into them they will be worthless. On the other hand, you can make only ten jumps, but if you do them with all your heart, they may inspire somebody. That inspiration will come back to you, bringing true satisfaction, joy, loftiness and ease."

—Tatyana Lebedeva (Russia), 3-time World Champion in triple jump,
Olympic gold and silver medallist in long jump

Become Disciplined in Your Training by Loving It

When you love to do something, it is not difficult to be disciplined. For instance, I will go to the gym today and I am really looking forward to it! As a professional athlete, the longest break I have taken were four days in a row. This, in over 30 years of weight-training and I don't intend to change that in the future. I can proudly say, 'I love training!'

"When I train, I concentrate and focus on my goals; I visualise them and I don't let myself be obstructed by any external factors. If you want to achieve great things in life or in sports, you need inner peace. That special state of mind will fire your workouts and help you in any endeavour you will undertake."

—**François Gay** (Switzerland), Natural Mr. Universe
and Natural Masters Mr. Olympia

The Art of Discipline

An athlete is an artist. An artist is he who has disciplined his life to discover the one Truth that manifests itself in various ways. The supreme art is a disciplined life. He who has disciplined his life is a great discoverer of truth, light, beauty, peace and bliss.

In order to become a good athlete, one has to discipline one's life considerably. One has to get up early in the morning to practise, and one has to practise hard again at noon or in the evening. One cannot become friends with lethargy, indolence and lack of punctuality. So the athlete's disciplined life is already veritable proof that he is an artist.

The athlete already has a sense of discipline – the discipline of the body. The discipline of the physical consciousness is of paramount importance, for the physical discipline takes a very long time to achieve. Through prayer and meditation we can easily discipline the psychic consciousness, the mental consciousness and the vital consciousness. But it takes a very long time to discipline the physical consciousness, because the physical in us is like a mischievous monkey. It takes a very long time to establish a disciplined peace in our physical consciousness. So the athlete who has achieved this discipline in his outer life is undoubtedly an artist from the spiritual point of view.

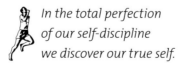

In the total perfection of our self-discipline we discover our true self.

Cosmic Energy

We can draw upon the cosmic energy by entering into our deeper consciousness, the all-pervading consciousness, which is here, there, everywhere. There are various types of "consciousness" in the spiritual worlds. It is the inner consciousness, the inmost consciousness, that touches the springs of the cosmic energy. If we can have a free access to our inmost consciousness, the cosmic energy is bound to come to the fore if you go deep within, it comes like a spring, a never-failing spring. And when it comes, it permeates the whole body.

We have more than 86,000 subtle nerves, but there are three principal nerves. They are called *Ida*, *Pingala* and *Sushumna*. One of the three has a very close connection with the cosmic energy. It can draw energy from the universe into itself in boundless measure in no time. He who knows how to concentrate and how to meditate well can have a free access to this cosmic energy, which originated along with the Cosmic Vision of God.

We have to know that physical energy has only one source, and that source is spiritual energy. As long as we remain in the body-consciousness, we are not aware of this. But when we go deep within, we see that spiritual energy is the source of physical, vital and mental energy.

There is a specific place where you receive all your strength, energy and determination. That place is your heart and your soul. Try to feel that all your strength, all your determination and willpower is in one particular place, here inside your heart.

Your determination has to have a connection with a deeper source. The outer mental discipline, the physical or vital discipline, cannot succeed unless and until it is backed by the soul's adamantine will-power.

Breathe In Energy

While you are running – especially when you are tired – you are much more conscious of your breathing. You are more aware of when you are inhaling and when you are exhaling. While running, when you inhale, you can consciously invoke divine energy to energise you. This divine energy energises the willing reality in you and illumines the unlit reality in you.

•••

Another way to overcome lethargy is by repeating 'Supreme' as fast as possible. You do not have to shout at the top of your lungs, but you have to be able to hear it; do not do it in silence. You can be seated in your room or walking in a silent place where nobody is going to hear you, but you should not do it while lying down.

While you are chanting 'Supreme', imagine everything that is inside you, starting with your toes. Think of your muscles, nerves, blood or anything that you want, and try to feel that the Supreme is entering into that particular part of your body. Then move to other parts of your body. You do not have to see what is inside your legs or your heart or your brain. Only imagine that something is there, and that that very thing is being touched by the word 'Supreme'. If lethargy has already stationed itself inside your knee or shoulder or somewhere else, that portion of the being has to be touched by the very presence of the Supreme. Each time you say 'Supreme', chanting as fast as possible, try to feel that the Power of the Supreme, the Life of the Supreme and the Divinity of the Supreme are entering into you.

Maintaining Freshness in Your Training

A way to sustain freshness and enthusiasm in our training is to have a sense of a clear, meaningful and fruitful goal. If we keep in mind this meaningful and fruitful goal, then enthusiasm and freshness will automatically dawn. If we value the goal, then the goal itself will give us enthusiasm and freshness. In order to overcome reluctance, we have to have a goal and we have to try to reach that goal.

•••

If you do not get enough joy from running, then bring some variety into your running. Do not run at the same speed or for the same distance every day. Every day change the distance or change the speed.

Every day must come to you as a new hope, a new promise, a new aspiration, a new energy, a new thrill and a new delight. Tomorrow will dawn and you have already seen thousands of days. If you think that tomorrow will be another day like those which you have already seen, then you will make no progress. You have to feel that tomorrow will be something absolutely new that you are going to create in your life.

Daring enthusiasm
And abiding cheerfulness
Can accomplish everything on earth
Without fail.

Should we run even when we are extremely tired?

As a rule, when we are extremely tired it is not advisable to run, for it will not help us in any way. At that time, running will be nothing but fatigue and self-destruction, and it will leave in our mind a bitter taste. But sometimes, even when we are not extremely tired, we feel that we are. At that time we are not actually physically tired. We are only mentally tired or emotionally tired, but the mind convinces us that we are physically tired. Our human lethargy is so clever! It acts like a rogue, a perfect rogue, and we get tremendous joy by offering compassion to our body. We make all kinds of justifications for the body's lethargy and make ourselves feel that the body deserves rest. So we have to be sincere to ourselves. If we really feel extremely tired, then we should not run. But we have to make sure that it is not our lethargic mind, our lethargic vital or our lethargic physical consciousness that is making us feel that we are extremely tired. This kind of tricky cleverness we have to conquer.

With our imagination-power we can challenge the tricky mind and win. We weaken ourselves by imagining that we are weak. Again, we can strengthen ourselves by imagining that we are strong. Our imagination often compels us to think we cannot do something or cannot say something. We often use imagination in a wrong direction. So instead of letting imagination take us backwards, we should use it to take us forward toward our goal.

The Heart Is Your Boss

Do not allow your mind to be your boss. You be the boss of your mind. Suppose one day you have taken rest. Then the mind will tell you that you have not practised for many days. All kinds of worries and anxieties will come to you and make you feel that you have taken many days rest. The mind may tell you that you have lost a little capacity or that you are not eager any more, you are not sincere any more, you are not serious any more. This roguish mind can tell you the following day that had you been very sincere, had you been very serious, then you would have practised yesterday as well. By saying that you are not serious and you are insincere, the mind is weakening you.

At that time you have to become the boss of your mind. The final judge has to be the heart. Whatever you do, the heart will say you did the right thing. If you stop after fifteen throws, the heart will say you did absolutely the right thing. The mind will say, "No, I should have done two or three more. Then I would have done better." But if you had done more, perhaps you would have injured yourself instead of doing better. So do not listen to the mind at all. Whatever you do, do happily and cheerfully. The day you are taking rest, feel that that is absolutely the right thing for you. The day you practise, feel that you are doing absolutely the right thing. Whatever you do, feel that you are doing absolutely the right thing. While you are doing something, if you think that you are not doing the right thing, the mind will take away all your joy, enthusiasm, eagerness and readiness.

Your happiness is your strength. Happiness will give you confidence; confidence will give you happiness. If you are doing the high jump or anything else, feel that you are doing it to make yourself happy. Whatever you do, do it happily. Do not have any regrets: "Oh, I should have done this; I should have done that." No, whatever you have done, feel that that is absolutely the right thing. That will give you joy. Once you do it, feel that you have done your best. If you say, "I should have done something else," it will weaken you. Then you will not be able to do your other events well. Always do everything well and say, "I have done the right thing. If I have taken rest, it was absolutely necessary. If I have not taken rest, it is because it was not necessary." Always convince your mind with happiness, happiness.

Rest and Sleep

There is a yogic method of getting rest. In one second you can take the rest of fifteen minutes, half an hour or even more. How can you get that kind of rest? When you go to sleep at night, feel that your whole body from head to foot has become a sea of peace. You have become peace itself. Consciously try to feel that you are not the body, but an infinite expanse of peace. When you can consciously feel this peace, you will see that your physical body has merged with it and totally disappeared in the sea of peace. If you can do this exercise effectively, you will need very little sleep.

Early in the morning when you find it difficult to get up, try to feel that your entire body, from head to foot, represents a sea of peace. Feel that you have become peace itself, that you embody peace within and without. Try to feel your physical frame consciously, but at the same time feel that you are an infinite expanse of peace. Peace can act like dynamic strength. You feel that when the body is active and moving to and fro, you have strength; but real strength exists in inner peace, not in outer action. When you possess peace in infinite measure, you possess the source of ordinary dynamic energy. If you call upon dynamic energy, which is inside you in the form of peace, then you can get up easily.

Meditation brings down peace. This peace energises the entire body. When your whole body is surcharged with peace, you do not need so many hours of rest. Sometimes two hours of rest will give you ample energy. Again, sometimes you may be in bed for hours and hours and not get any real rest. The number of hours that you sleep is not the important thing, but rather how well you sleep. If you find that it is difficult to get up in the morning, you have to know that during eight hours of sleep perhaps you have not had even one hour of good sleep.

Maintaining Your Enthusiasm

In short distances – from one hundred metres to a mile – it is easy to maintain enthusiasm. You get a burst of energy or inspiration and you go. But for long distances, to maintain enthusiasm is very difficult. There are many, many ways to keep your enthusiasm when you are getting tired in long-distance, but here are two ways that are particularly effective.

While running, do not think of yourself as twenty-five or thirty years old. Only think of yourself as being six or seven years old. At the age of six or seven, a child does not sit, he just runs here and there. So imagine the enthusiasm of a young child and identify yourself not with the child but with the source of his enthusiasm. This is one way.

Another secret way, if you are running long distance, is to identify yourself with ten or even twenty runners who are ahead of you. Only imagine the way they are breathing in and breathing out. Then, while you are inhaling, feel that you are breathing in their own breath and that the energy of the twenty runners is entering into you. Then, while you are exhaling, feel that all twenty runners are breathing out your tiredness and lack of enthusiasm. So secretly you will breathe in the breath of twenty runners at a time.

This energy which you get, which is nothing but enthusiasm, will let you go ten steps forward. But you have to remember that you are breathing in their breath, their inspiration and determination, and not their tiredness. You have to feel that their breath is like clean, distilled water. If you think of someone who is dying, that person's breath will not help you. But if you think of someone who is running faster than you, his energy will help you. You are not stealing it; only you are taking in the spiritual energy that is all around him and inside him, just as it is inside you. But because he is running faster, you are more conscious of it in him.

Increasing Speed

To a great extent, speed in running starts with the mind. You have to develop more imagination. Imagine that you are running fast and appreciate your speed. Then let the thrill and joy that you get from your imagination inundate you. This joy will increase your speed. You can also think of some people who really do run fast and try to identify yourself with them.

This is all based on imagination. Of course, you can take quite a few exercises to increase your speed. Limbering and stretching exercises will help a little. But imagination plays a great role in increasing speed.

Strengthening the Legs

If your legs get tired from standing all day, there are two exercises that are very good to strengthen them. One exercise develops the knee muscles. You sit on the floor with one leg straight, and the other leg bent with the knee up, both hands on your hips. Then you switch, bending the straight leg and straightening the bent leg. Then keep switching.

The other exercise is to do a deep knee bend on one leg, with the other leg out in front of you, and then stand up again, still keeping one leg in front of you. First you do it with a flat foot, then on your toe. If you can do it three or four times, your legs will have tremendous strength from top to bottom.

Ups and Downs

Your running capacity changes every day because every day you are in a different consciousness. One day you feel light. One day you feel heavy. One day you feel inspiration and another day you feel no inspiration. On a slow day, if you want to maintain the same joy that you have when you are running well, you can play a trick on yourself. Imagine that instead of being forced to run at a ten-minute pace [6:13 min/km] that day, you decided to run at that pace.

If you feel that you are compelled to run slowly, then you will feel that your freedom has gone away, and you do not want to be anybody's slave. But if you feel that it was you who commanded your body to go at a ten-minute pace, then you won't feel miserable. Right from the beginning, if you feel that it was your decision to run at that speed, you will be as happy as if you were running at a seven-minute pace [4:21 min/km].

If your progress in one field
Is obstructed,
Go another way.
There are so many ways
Open to you
If you look within.
Only do not give up
The idea of progress.

Life is not always smooth sailing; it goes up and down. The main thing is to get satisfaction. While running, when you touch your peak you are very happy. When you are unable to reach your peak, you should not feel that it is your fault. It is not that you have deliberately injured yourself. You have not said to your body, "I fed you so many times, now I want to starve you." If you are deliberately enjoying your lack of speed or lack of enthusiasm then you are to be blamed. But if circumstances have led you to this condition, please try to maintain your equanimity and peace of mind. Feel that you are going through a phase that may last for three or four weeks, but that eventually it will pass.

While you are in this deplorable condition, try to think of the summit which you reached two or three weeks earlier, and try to remember the joy that you felt. Then you will see that the joy you got from your previous achievements will carry you through, and very soon you will not only reach but transcend your previous height. You are not fooling yourself; you are only bringing happiness into your system, and this happiness is confidence. Again, confidence itself is happiness. Try to feel that your problem is just a small obstacle, a hurdle that you will soon overcome. Then you will be able to diminish the frustration that you now feel. Once you diminish your frustration, again in a week or so you will be able to regain your capacity. But if you maintain or increase your frustration, then the problem will linger. It may go on for two or three weeks.

Be determined to climb over each and every mountain-obstacle you encounter in your life.

One approach is to think of the hurdles that you face in life. Another approach is to think of the joy that you will get after crossing over the hurdles. When we have an obstacle – on the physical, vital, mental, psychic or spiritual plane – we can either approach the obstacle as an enemy, which everybody does, an obstacle race, a hindrance, or we can say: "Here is an opportunity to strengthen my capacity. This is an obstacle; I will overcome it."

Maintaining Good Health

It is one thing to have good health and another thing to deliberately maintain good health. Unless you are consciously keeping good health, at any moment you may be attacked by some forces. It is like having a large amount of money without knowing about it. If you are not conscious of it, you may easily lose it. If you are not conscious that you have a flower, you are likely to lose it. Anything that you have must have some place in your awareness. You may have good physical health, but perhaps in two months time you have not thought of your body once, let alone tried to increase the strength of your legs or arms or to get some extra capacity.

Unless you touch something every day, it does not shine. Often I have told people to touch the furniture in their homes every day. As soon as you touch something, it gets new life. If you are aware of something, immediately it shines and gets a new luminosity. If you have good health, if you touch your health every day, it gets new life. By giving attention to something, you give new life to it.

Why do I injure myself when I start doing more sports?

When you enter into the physical world – playing tennis or other things – you do not give value to the physical as such. You remain in the mind. A portion of your existence you throw into the game and another portion you keep totally in the mind-world. It is like cutting yourself in half. You are keeping your body on the first floor, but your consciousness is always on the upper floor, in the mind. If you can direct more of your mental energy into the physical when you play, this will not happen. You want to play; you want to win. But actually the concentration of the mind, the real concentration, is not in the physical itself. You know that you are playing tennis, but the concentration that the body needs from the mind is not there. There is a gap. The body without concentration from the mind is help-less. So, when you play, do not think of your mental work. Your mind may not be aware that it is thinking of the wrong thing, but it is one thing not to be aware of doing the wrong thing and another thing to concentrate consciously on the right thing. Inside you and all around you there are many beings. Because there is a gap between the mind's concentration and the physical activity, these beings can attack the physical. They need not actually be wrong forces, but they may create unfortunate experiences in life.

Why do we get injuries for no apparent reason?

There is always a reason, either in the inner world or in the outer world. In the inner world, if something is dislocated – if your consciousness has descended or if some hostile forces have attacked – you get an injury. Sometimes you are totally innocent, but the wrong forces, the malicious forces which are hovering around, can cause injury. Again, sometimes in the inner world or in the thought-world you have done something wrong, and this can also cause an injury. Thought can be more destructive than a hydrogen bomb. Wrong thoughts, which are so destructive, may come and attack you, especially your physical, which is in ignorance most of the time. The wrong forces find it very easy to attack the plane which is fast asleep, because they will encounter no opposition there. So, in the inner world either your consciousness has descended because of wrong thoughts, or some hostile force has attacked you, and that is why you get an injury which you cannot see any reason for.

No Pain, No Gain?

Not only bodybuilders but also many other athletes are of the opinion, "No pain, no gain." Either I can use my wisdom-light or my stupidity-height. If we say that only by hurting ourselves can we improve ourselves, it is almost like saying that we should overeat in order to strengthen ourselves, that we should eat voraciously so that overnight we can become stronger than the strongest. That is not possible! Slowly and steadily we shall try to increase our capacities, not by leaps and bounds, which can cause us injuries.

I find it difficult to accept the theory that physical pain is unavoidable in order to improve. True, we may at times get pain as we struggle with an exercise or with heavy weights. But that is a totally different matter. If we deliberately torture our body beyond its limited capacity with the hope of becoming stronger overnight, then there is every possibility that the body will revolt. This kind of training will tell upon our health.

How can we spiritually heal injuries?

It is a matter of inner capacity. One kind of capacity is to heal the injury by bringing down peace and light from Above. Another kind of capacity is to ignore the pain altogether. During your meditation, if all of a sudden you have intense aspiration, then you can bring down more light from above to cure your injury. But you have to do this consciously during your meditation. If during the day you casually say, "Oh, how I wish I didn't have any pain!" that will be useless. But while you are meditating, if you suddenly remember your pain, that is the time to pray and bring down more light.

Everything has to depend on prayer and meditation. Again, outer therapy is also of supreme need. Of course, the most important thing is the inner prayer. But it is like a boxer using two hands. With one hand you cannot do everything. You should take as much help from medical science as possible, and at the same time you have to think of our spiritual science, which is prayer and meditation. They have to go side by side.

The Natural Way

I pray to God that the things that are unnatural, the things that are not healthy, the things that are damaging to the physical or subtle body, people will give up as soon as possible. The drugs that are making people stronger than the strongest on the physical plane will definitely have immediate side effects on the inner plane. On the physical plane also, slowly and steadily they will have very severe side effects. So my ardent prayer to man and God is for people to use nothing unnatural, for these undivine things eventually will destroy them. These things may bring immediate success but they can destroy the potentialities and infinite capacities that each individual has, to do something not only for himself but for the entire humanity. Somebody takes steroids and he feels that it is his individual problem. He does not realise that he is part of humanity. If you do something right, then you help humanity. If you do something wrong, do not think that only you as an individual will be affected. No, everybody will be affected. By doing something wrong, we bring down the progress of humanity.

It is quite possible to be among the best in the world without using steroids. There will come a time in the near future when athletes will be able to break world records and better the world standards without using any drugs.

Nature embodies the cosmic energy. This cosmic energy is infinitely stronger than any man-made chemicals. This energy comes from the ultimate Source and it leads us to the ultimate Source while fulfilling and satisfying us along the way. Chemicals and other artificial things will ultimately fail, for they are unnatural.

> What do you want to be? Do you want to be a winner in life and be healthy and be able to look at yourself in the mirror and say, 'This is me, I can be proud of myself'? Or do you want to be somebody who is taking lots of drugs, and is ruining his health just for a trophy? That's the choice you have.
>
> "My message is this: the natural way may take longer, and the road can be tougher, but at the end you will be glad you have taken this road."
>
> **—François Gay**

Coaching

My simple message that I can offer to coaches is to have a childlike heart, a oneness-heart with their students. They should try to feel constant oneness not only with their students' outer needs but also with their inner needs. Most coaches help their students outwardly, but inwardly they are unable to help. But if they pray and meditate along with their students while the students are performing, they can help their students considerably. Coaches should practise the prayer-life and meditation-life and also encourage their students to do the same. On the outer plane they have wisdom; they know much more than their students. But if they do not take help from their own inner resources and also help their students on the inner plane, then their students may not or cannot develop to their greatest potential. Coaches should dive deep within and bring to the fore their own inspiration, aspiration, dedication, determination and will-power and offer these capacities to their students. In that way the students and the coaches will work together in their inner lives of aspiration and their outer lives of dedication, and the success they have will be tremendous and will last forever.

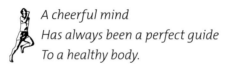

A cheerful mind
Has always been a perfect guide
To a healthy body.

CHAPTER NINE

Competition

There are only three winners:
The one who
  Competes with himself,
The one who
  Crosses the finish line first
And the one who
  Finishes the race.

Compete with Yourself

If you are competing with others, you have to remember that you are not competing with the person who is beside you or with those who are in front of you or behind you. You are only competing with yourself. Otherwise wrong ideas will come into your mind. Your attitude will be to defeat that person by hook or by crook. Then it is your destruction. But if you are only competing with others in order to run the fastest, to do your best, then whatever result comes, you will be happy.

Our philosophy is self-transcendence. I happen to be an athlete. Let us say I have reached a certain standard and I am very proud of myself. But the moment I look around, I will see that somebody else can defeat me easily. So if we enter into the world of competition and try to defeat the whole world, we will be doomed to disappointment. Perhaps this moment we will stand first, but the next moment there will be somebody else to defeat us. So in the world of competition there is no peace; always there is somebody who is better. But if we try to compete only with ourselves and continually improve our own standard, then we are always happy.

If you think at the starting line, you are going to have a terrible start. The calmest moments I ever had in competition was just before I started, the last five seconds. When they would say, 'Come to your mark, get in your blocks...,' this was when I had the most intense moments of meditation. I don't think of anything. I don't think of the race, what I have to do, my performance, what place I am going to come in. My mind goes completely blank so that I can listen to that gun. If you are thinking about something, then that comes before the sound of the gun. So there could be a million people and someone screaming in my ear and I wouldn't hear that. And it would be so peaceful and calm just listening for the sound of the gun. And I think that was one of the reasons I never false-started, because I never worried about that before the sound of the gun.

"You have to be an expert in concentration and meditation because you have to be able to focus on something when the time is very stressful. You have to be able to block out things that can clog your mind or change your thought process, and you have to also believe. Meditation has helped me to eliminate some of the problems that come as an athlete. Especially as a world-class athlete, there is a lot of pressure in competition. Meditation has helped me to eliminate a lot of the pressure through having faith and at the same time not worrying what other people are doing on the track. When I meditate I feel more relaxed and calm. That's the thing; it takes away the pressure. That's what I feel the most: peace and confidence.

"What other people call pressure, I call inspiration.

"At home I usually do my meditation and at the track I definitely say a prayer. Some days I prefer just to be calm and have a meditative consciousness, but I always say a prayer. This is something I make sure before every competition. I don't think of the race; it is more than that. I pray for all the athletes, that no one gets injured and all stay healthy. In mental training you focus on yourself to beat the others, whereas in meditation you focus on yourself to give the best you can.

"If you have the strength coming from within and the power coming from within, if you can achieve it, then you can achieve any goal that you set for yourself."

—Carl Lewis

Do not enter
Into the world of comparison.
Just dare to better yourself
Every day, without fail!

I am happy because
I have realised the truth
That the most important thing
In my life
Is self-improvement.

Joy Is in Progress, Not in Success

We run the fastest when we do not look to this side or that side. If we let ourselves become distracted by thinking of the person who is either beside us or behind us but not at the goal itself, we will fail to reach the goal. Always think of the goal and your problem will be solved.

Always there should be a goal. Having a goal does not mean that we have to try to defeat the world's top runners, far from it. There is something which is very essential, necessary and inevitable, which we call progress. Our goal should be our own progress, and progress itself is the most illumining experience.

I feel improvement is necessary in order for us to make progress. In this world we are happy only when we make progress. If we are satisfied with what we have right now, and we do not want to go forward, then we will not be happy.

Joy is in progress, not in success. Success ends our journey, but progress has no end. When you have a fixed goal and you reach it, that is your success. After that, you are finished. But if you do not have a fixed goal, if your goal is going higher all the time, then you will constantly make progress, and you will get the greatest satisfaction.

So do not be satisfied with success. Aspire only for progress. Each time you make progress, that is your real success.

> Believe me, the joy that comes from 'going beyond' is the most incredible feeling in the world. I have felt it many times. And I have enjoyed watching others experience it. The ultimate joy comes from performing one's absolute best, no matter one's order of finish.
>
> "For me the Olympics are embodied in one of the favourite passages from Sri Chinmoy: 'All the athletes should bear in mind that they are competing not with other athletes but with their own capacities. Whatever they have already achieved, they have to go beyond.'"
>
> **—Carl Lewis**

Why Compete?

At times we ask if it is worth taking such trouble, time and concern. But we do everything in life in order to achieve satisfaction. We will not do anything unnecessary if we do not see or feel that there will be satisfaction at the end of our achievement. This satisfaction can be either fleeting or lasting.

There are many athletes who get inspiration and enthusiasm only when they compete with others. I cannot blame them. If someone is in a position to compete with somebody else, that means he is inspired, he is enthusiastic. If he is competing with someone, then he can bring to the fore his utmost capacity. Otherwise he may be lethargic. He may not practise daily. The physical discipline in his life may come into existence only when he knows that he has to compete with somebody else. Otherwise, he may not take these physical exercises seriously.

Our aim should not be to surpass others but to constantly surpass our own previous achievements. We cannot properly evaluate our own capacity unless we have some standard of comparison. Therefore, we compete not for the sake of defeating others but in order to bring forward our own capacity. Our best capacity comes forward only when there are other people around us. They inspire us to bring forward our utmost capacity, and we inspire them to bring forward their utmost capacity.

If you participate in races, it will add to your strength and determination in the inner world. While practising every day, you usually do not have the same kind of determination that you have when you are running a race. While you are in a race, even if you are a poor runner, you are determined to do your best, so you collect some inner strength and determination. This determination immediately enters into the Universal Consciousness and, like wildfire, it spreads. Then, somebody running in Africa or Australia or in some other part of the world will all of a sudden feel a burst of energy, which is coming from you and nobody else.

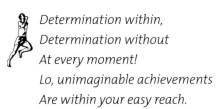

Determination within,
Determination without
At every moment!
Lo, unimaginable achievements
Are within your easy reach.

Why do we get more satisfaction from training than from racing?

You get more satisfaction from your training than from your racing because when you train, you have more oneness with your inner life, which embodies infinite satisfaction. When you race, you are competing with others because you want to defeat them. The challenging spirit that comes in competition quite often suffers from anxiety, worry, doubt, hesitation and despair. When you are just practising, however, you are performing before the most intimate members of your

Training in the Swiss Alps. *A happy biker during a challenging bike ride in the Swiss Alps.*

family – your body, vital, mind, heart and soul. In fact, these intimate members of your own being are practising and performing with you, in you and for you. It is totally a family entertainment.

While practising, you are consciously working to transcend your capacities. At that time, you are listening to the message of the ever-transcending Beyond, and this message itself is complete satisfaction. But when you compete against others, you are more concerned with victory than with self-transcendence. Naturally, at that time hesitation, anxiety and doubt have a free access to your heart and mind, and you do not and cannot have satisfaction.

But when you practise, you and your aspiration, you and your dedication, you and your eagerness to increase your capacities work together for your improvement and perfection. And from improvement and perfection, you are bound to get abiding satisfaction.

Because of the feeling of separativity in the mind, we may get fleeting satisfaction when we defeat others. But perhaps quite a few times during your practice you have had more illumining and more fulfilling satisfaction, for practice carries the message of oneness and self-transcendence, whereas competition carries the message of division and supremacy.

When there is a feeling of supremacy, you can forget about harmony.

Maintaining Your Poise Before a Race

Before the 1996 Olympic trials, my friend, Sri Chinmoy, called from New York to wish me well in the trials. He also offered this advice: 'Find your own time to be quiet. There will be so many activities, so many distractions, so many people talking around you and about you. You must not allow others to drain your heart energy.' It was vintage Sri Chinmoy. His thoughts are so often connected straight to the heart. They flow from the heart. They lead to the heart. In closing, Sri Chinmoy suggested that I find one hour a day to be alone in silence. No television. No telephone. No teammates or friends. Just me and my thoughts and a chance to connect with a higher power."

—Carl Lewis

> I start preparing and concentrating on the event not an hour or two before it, but a day or two in advance. I try, as much as I can, to dive inside, to socialise less. At press conferences, I try not to be too open. I save my emotions, keep them inside, otherwise, when I speak from my heart, it takes all my energy away. When I stay inside, I ponder over serious things, I can mix up only with dear and near ones. I try to keep my heart burning and my mind cool. At such moments, I like to discuss philosophy, the goal of life. It allows me to keep concentrating on the competition."
>
> **—Tatyana Lebedeva**

Observing the Competition

We have to feel that we are not the doer, that the Supreme is the only Doer. We have to feel that the inspiration for the action is not ours, and the fruit of the action is not ours. If we can feel that we are just the instruments of the Supreme, our actions can be perfect.

Nervousness comes only when we feel that we are the doers. If Somebody else is the Doer, then we are just the witnesses. It is up to Him whether we are successful or not. We have only to be good instruments. But if we feel that we are doing it ourselves, then we are in trouble.

Before the race starts, meditate most soulfully for five minutes. Try to make yourself feel that you are not the competitor, but that Somebody else is competing in and through you. You are only the witness, the spectator. Since Somebody else is competing, you are at perfect liberty to watch and enjoy. While you are competing, sometimes it is very difficult to enjoy the race. Either the competitive spirit or frustration is killing you, or your body is not abiding by your mental will and you feel that you are literally dying. So many problems arise.

But before you start, if you can convince yourself that you are a divine observer and that Somebody else is competing in you, through you and for you, then fear, doubt, frustration, anxiety and other negative forces will not be able to assail your mind. Once these thoughts occupy the mind, they try to enter into the vital and then into the physical. Once they enter into the physical, they create tension, and this makes you lose all your power of concentration. But if you feel that you are not the competitor, if you feel that you are observing the competition from the beginning to the end, then there will be no tension, and these forces will not attack you. This is the only way to overcome these forces and maintain the highest type of concentration from the beginning to the end.

This is what I do. As a runner I am useless, but right at the beginning I try to become an instrument and make myself feel that Somebody else, my Beloved Supreme, is running in and through me. Right at the beginning of the race I offer my gratitude-heart to the Supreme, and at the end, after I finish the race, I also offer my gratitude. If I can offer my soulful gratitude to my Inner Pilot before the race and after the race also, then there can be no frustration, no decline of aspiration. The aspiration and power of concentration will remain the same throughout the race.

Our heart's gratitude
Produces a sleepless energy
Which helps us bring about success
In each and every aspect of our life.

→

A peaceful moment. Sri Chinmoy meditates before a race.

No Anxiety

Anxiety and alertness are two different dynamic energies. With anxiety, you are always worrying about others and comparing yourself to them. But with alertness, you simply want to do the best you can. When the starter is about to fire the gun, you should be alert but not anxious. You should not say, "If he comes in first and I come in last, no harm." No, let him do his best; but you also have to do your best, and this requires alertness.

When you run, try to feel that you are the only runner in the race. Before the gun goes off, do not think of others; think only of yourself – that you are going to run at your own fastest speed. You want to see your capacity. So you will remain alert, but you will not think of others. In this way there can be no anxiety.

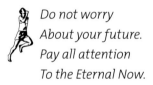

Do not worry
About your future.
Pay all attention
To the Eternal Now.

Relax

Relaxation is of supreme importance for all athletes. First you have to relax psychically, in your heart. Then you have to relax mentally, then vitally and then physically. If you are relaxed, when you, as an individual, want to do something, then you get a force inside your heart, mind, vital and physical. You are also getting a force inside your soul. Five strong forces, inner forces, are helping you secretly. Relaxation means help from the inner, secret world. So in everything you do, relaxation is of paramount importance. But it must be relaxation. It is not a matter of enjoying lethargy. Relaxation can take place sooner than the soonest if you can make your mind calm, quiet, vacant. If you can make your mind calm and quiet, you will see relaxation of the various parts of your being can be achieved very quickly.

Relaxation *starts inside your heart and mind – as this runner is doing*
prior to the start of the Rockland Lake State Park Marathon (USA).

Purity Wins

Suppose there are two athletes who, on the physical plane, have the same standard. If you are pure and the other is impure, what will happen? If you really have
the same standard, then definitely you will be able to defeat the impure one. As
soon as you touch the shot, you will be able to control your vital thoughts, mental
thoughts and physical thoughts. But when the other one holds it, he will look
around to see if others are looking at him. When he is thinking of the audience,
some of his strength goes away. As soon as he identifies himself with the audience,
what he gets is their worries, anxieties and tension. But when you are throwing, as soon as you hold the shot, there is only you and the Supreme. You are not

allowing your vital to come forward. You do not open the physical door. You do not open the mental door. Purity is your bodyguard. It does not allow any wrong force to come. You have no idea who is good, who is bad, who is your enemy. Your purity-guard is very strict. It will not allow anything wrong to enter into your mind. So if one athlete has the same capacity as someone else, the one who is purer is bound to win, because he will not allow himself to be attacked by outside forces at the time of competition.

How to Keep Calm When Problems Arise

Either you have to be clever or you have to become inwardly oriented. If you are clever, you can say to yourself that it could be infinitely worse. By saying this, a kind of relaxation and mental peace or poise comes. But if you are inwardly oriented, then before the race you can meditate most powerfully for 15 or 20 minutes. This will enable you to acquire tremendous mental power. When you have this mental power, the problems that may arise during the race will not be able to disturb you at all. Your mental power will be able to silence the power of the so-called problems before and during the event.

How to Keep the Pace When Running Alone

At that time you have to use your stopwatch. If you know you can do under a five-minute pace for seven miles, then try to increase your capacity. You may be ahead of the other runners, but you are not ahead of your best possible time. Suppose you were planning to run at a 4:30 pace [2:48 min/km], but everyone is behind you, so you are not getting any inspiration or challenge. Just look at your stopwatch and think of it as another rival or competitor. Then you will be inspired to run faster.

When We Feel Like Dropping Out of a Race

We have to use our wisdom at every moment. Sometimes we are physically tired. Sometimes we are mentally tired. Sometimes we are emotionally tired. Sometimes we are tired without any rhyme or reason. Often our mental lethargy makes us feel that we will not be able to complete the race or, if we complete the race, nothing special is going to happen. There are so many ways in which our mind can convince us that it is useless and unnecessary to continue. The mind makes us feel, "I am just killing myself without any specific purpose."

If mental lethargy or our own unwillingness tortures us, we must not surrender to these wrong forces. Our motto is, "Never give up!" Only after we have given everything that we have and everything that we are can we give up if it is absolutely necessary. Otherwise, we are making the most deplorable mistake. Most of the time there is every possibility that we shall be able to arrive at our destination. And once we arrive at our destination, it is we who will be the happiest and the proudest person.

> Even when you feel you cannot achieve your goal, never drop out of a race. When you drop out once, you will do it again. You have to accept that you can run a bad race and know that sport is not only winning medals or being number one. I am a strong believer that a man is not only measured by his outer performances but also by his inner achievements. Finishing a bad going race and to accept the outcome can be a big achievement. Sport is not the whole life. A bad performance is always a new challenge."
>
> **—Paul Tergat**

The determination in your heroic effort
Will permeate your mind and heart
Even after your success or failure
Is long forgotten.

Going Beyond Winning and Losing

"When I look at the season like 1996, the ultimate goal for me was not necessarily to win the gold medal in the long jump. Obviously I was glad to do it, but the ultimate goal was to win the gold medal in effort. Even if you win (I have seen some very shallow wins, but some very happy losses), ultimately, you want to feel like you gave what you had because then you can fulfil the only thing you could at the time: your best effort. That's really what it comes down to. This separates a lot of great athletes and great people in our society. They are the ones who can allow themselves to be separate from 'wins and losses', the good and the bad races, and just say, 'All of this and actually everything I do, is ultimately out of my control. I can just do the best I can and allow something to happen; I can feel fulfilled in other ways.'

"What you have to do is to prepare yourself physically, emotionally and spiritually to accept what happens that day. That is what a lot of people are afraid to do, to say, 'Well, I have done everything I can do. Right this very moment all I can do is perform; that part is out of my hands,' but a lot of people try to control. They are the ones that never really achieve success to the level that they can achieve because they think that you can control the performances; you can control what you do that day. They try to control too much instead of allowing a lot of it to just happen. That makes a big difference.

"You see athletes that are so driven by their performance – 'I have to break this time' – that it seems that they are never happy. They may break world records, because they are controlling the performance and not allowing more than just 'I'm faster than you' to occur. So it's far more than just 'I'm across the line first.' There's a process of 'Did I dedicate myself to perform? Did I work as hard as I can? Did I give a hundred per cent effort? Did I allow myself to accept everything that can help me become the best I can be?'"

—Carl Lewis

Making history. *With this winning long jump at the 1996 Olympics in Atlanta, Carl Lewis joined discus-thrower Al Oerter, the only other athlete to have won four gold medals in one event.*
(Photo © Abakash)

Defeat can be a reality which is secretly preparing us to run the fastest.

As children, we learn how to walk only after repeated falls. We become a fast runner after losing the race many times. We become good wrestlers by being defeated many times. If I feel sad when I observe someone else winning a race, this will not help me. But if I can appreciate his speed, automatically some of his capacity will enter into me. Through sincere appreciation we gain capacity. When I see that somebody is running the fastest, I really feel that I am that person. If you can identify with other people's successes, instead of envying them, you will get a great deal more joy out of life. And of course, if you can identify with their defeats as well, you will learn sympathy and kindness as well as enriching your own experience.

If you meditate, even when you lose you can easily feel the same joy that the winner feels. And something more, you can feel the joy of the winner as your own, very own. It is not self-deception. Meditation gives you the power of oneness. So the winner and the loser can easily become one on the strength of their meditation. Also, if you are the winner, on the strength of your meditation if you can for a few seconds establish your sympathetic oneness with the loser, you will not only get the joy from your victory but you will also get added joy. You will increase your happiness by becoming one with the loser. Your sympathy and concern will offer you great satisfaction, a kind of satisfaction that you will not get by winning.

Whoever can
Soulfully and powerfully
Smile the oneness-smile
Before the game,
During the game
And after the game
Is undoubtedly the real winner.

An athlete practises seriously for three or four months, and then during the competition he has to show his capacity. If he does poorly, he may think, "Oh, I made such sacrifices for so many months. Now what a deplorable result!" But it was not a sacrifice. He was only giving for a period of time, and now he is receiving the result in the form of an experience. The seeker who recognises his inner oneness with the rest of the world will not feel sad and miserable if he does poorly. This kind of experience – both success and failure – is absolutely necessary for everybody in every walk of life.

From the spiritual point of view, we say there is no such thing as sacrifice when there is a feeling of oneness. If there is a sense of separativity, there is always sacrifice; otherwise, it is all oneness, all oneness. It is all part of God's Cosmic Game that I do this and you do that. There is no I, there is no you, there is no winner or loser. It is all one reality, a oneness-reality.

Competition is good,
Provided it is the competition
Of self-transcendence
And not the competition
Of ego-demonstration.

Each time we challenge someone, we inwardly weaken ourselves. But if we establish our oneness with someone, then we get that person's strength. When you establish your oneness with others, immediately you expand your consciousness. If someone does something well, you have to feel that it is you who have done it. Others should also feel the same when you do something significant. Whenever any individual does something very well, we have to feel that it is our conscious inspiration and aspiration that have enabled that individual to achieve this success. If we always have an attitude of teamwork, then we will be able to conquer the ego. To conquer the ego is to gain boundless freedom. The human ego can never, under any circumstances experience true inner joy. True inner joy is self-created. It does not depend on outer circumstances or outer achievements.

•••

An athlete can have peace on the strength of his oneness. Before he starts his competition, he can just take a fleeting second to feel: "No matter who is first, I will be equally happy, for whoever wins is my brother or sister. If I did not run or jump, there would be no competition, so that person could not be a winner. Again, if I win, it is only because others have also run and jumped."

If we think of oneness before we do something, if we can maintain this feeling of oneness while we are acting and also at the end of our action, then there will always be peace. From the beginning to the end, we have to sing the song of oneness. Let us say we are running in a marathon. There are thousands of other people going to the same destination. Someone else may be first and I may be last. But if I have established my oneness with the other runners, then I will be equally happy because they are all part and parcel of my life. I will not feel miserable that one part of me has reached the goal before another part. Without oneness, no matter what we do, we are unhappy. Even when we are successful, the joy we get does not last.

The glories of the outer life
Will eventually fade away
Like the falling stars.

If I take both defeat and victory as an experience, then doubt cannot enter. If I am unable to do something, it is an experience, and if I am able to do it, this is another experience. So how can doubt come? I see the experience that I get from victory and the experience that I get from defeat as equally good experiences; therefore, doubt cannot torture me. Doubt tortures me only when I say, "What will happen to me if I do not do something, if I can not do something?" If I do not do something, the world is not going to dissolve. And if I do it, the world is not going to be saved. If I lose, the experience I am getting is coming from Above; and if I win, the experience is also coming from Above.

When we can see victory and defeat as equal, then there can be no doubt whatsoever. If I cannot do something, I am happy, and if I can do that thing, I am equally happy – because both are, after all, only experiences that I am getting, and these experiences my Inner Pilot is Himself having in and through me.

Do not think of failure; be cheerful. If you failed previously, feel that that day did not exist. Make your mind fresh and clean. Live with new hope and new promise.

The idea of failure is a most deplorable thing in one's life, whether in bodybuilding or in any other field. We must never cherish the idea of failure. We must always have the feeling that we shall succeed. There is no such thing as permanent failure. Failure is only temporary. Even if we fail today, tomorrow we are bound to succeed.

Failure is an experience which awakens us. Success is an experience which energises us to strive for a higher and greater success.

THE WINNER AND THE LOOSER

He is the great winner
Who wins.

He is the greater winner
Who is the cheerful loser.

He is the greatest winner
Who gives equal value
To victory and defeat.

He alone is the real loser
Who separates
Defeat from victory.

 If you want to be
A future success,
Then do not allow your mind
To dwell on the present defeat.

The Olympic Games

> Each of the Olympic Games is unique and very special. With time, you come to understand that it is not only the honour to participate and the victory that matters. Mainly, you compete with your own self.
>
> "Now I have a different motivation than before, when I was so eager to beat the others, to earn the money. Now sport for me is a possibility to transcend myself; it does not allow me to relax, it makes me go forward, only forward. It shows me that I really have the capacity to get over my shortcomings, to resist them, to conquer my laziness. May I have the capacity to overcome all the difficulties within and without!"
>
> **—Tatyana Lebedeva**

The very word 'Olympics' is, for me, a magnificent thrill, absolutely a universal thrill, and it raises the consciousness of humanity in the inner world. True, in the outer world we may notice some wrong forces, but in the inner world the Olympics is a great opportunity for the upliftment of human consciousness.

The Olympics are an unprecedented, auspicious, glorious and precious Greece-vision. And what is this vision? This vision is nothing other than world-happiness. Happiness is love bubbling forth into the newness and fulness of true life, illumining life and fulfilling life.

The Olympics means oneness – the oneness of nations. Like Socrates, we say, "I am not an Athenian; I am a universal man."

The presence of all the great athletes at the Olympics represents a great opportunity. When an athlete has to compete with the rest of the world, there is every opportunity and possibility that he will transcend his own capacities. This is what is of paramount importance, and not whether he defeats others or not. If we are one with the rest of the world, then we feel joy in others' joy and their sorrow is also our sorrow. But most of us have not yet attained that consciousness. So it is always advisable for the athlete to keep in mind that he is competing with his own previous record. If he can transcend his own achievement, then it will be a true gain and a true achievement for the whole world.

What is of paramount importance is the individual's attitude. The athlete has to feel that he is establishing a new record not for his own glory but in order to increase the capacity and improve the standard of the world. The winning athlete has to feel that he is representing all of humanity. Then, with a devoted and soulful heart, if he can soulfully offer his achievement to the Supreme Athlete, his Source, at that time he is doing absolutely the right thing. If this is his attitude then let him try his utmost to break world records. But if he wants to defeat the rest of the world only to bask in his own glory, then he is making a deplorable mistake.

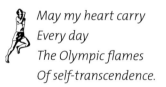

May my heart carry
Every day
The Olympic flames
Of self-transcendence.

When we win, we have to feel that it is the standard of humanity that has gone high. If I have defeated you, then I should not get malicious pleasure. Only I should say, "You and I are one. You are part and parcel of humanity and I am also part and parcel of humanity. So in my achievement, it is humanity's progress."

The Olympic athlete should feel that he is a member of the world-family, and his goal should be his own continuous progress. If he can continually transcend his own achievements, he is bound to achieve satisfaction, for progress is nothing short of satisfaction. The two go always together. If he cares only for success, then even if he succeeds he will not get abiding joy. For in the twinkling of an eye he will look around and see his achievements being shattered here or elsewhere. But his own progress is like a seed that eventually becomes a sapling and then a giant banyan tree which will give him a continuous sense of satisfaction. When he is progressing, at that time he is growing, he is glowing and, like a river, he is constantly flowing to his Vastness-Source, the Sea of Oneness.

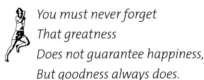

You must never forget
That greatness
Does not guarantee happiness,
But goodness always does.

I appreciate and admire the Olympic Games because they are raising the world standard. Right now the athletes are trying to defeat each other. For the time being this is good. If they did not have a competitive spirit, then they would be at home sleeping. It is better to be active and dynamic than lazy and useless. It is better to be moving forward than standing still. While moving forward, if they want to try to go ahead of those who are moving with them, no harm. Although this is not the highest way, it is far better than remaining inactive and lethargic.

After some time they will see that there is a higher way of looking at sports. If victory is the only goal, then the athletes can never find happiness, for even if they win today, tomorrow somebody else will come along and take away their glory. Real happiness can never be found in separating ourselves from others. Real happiness comes only in feeling our oneness with others, even if they defeat us.

We are all members of a family. If your brother defeats you in running, you are not miserable, because he is your brother. Again, if you defeat him in swimming because you have more capacity in that sport, your brother is not going to feel miserable. He will say, "It is my brother who has done it, so it is all right." Like that, if all the athletes can feel that they belong to one family, then they will be happy no matter who wins.

Regardless of who wins on the sports ground, each one should try to excel in his own life by competing with himself and going forward according to his own capacity to his destined goal. In this way each individual will all the time make progress and achieve greater and greater perfection. True happiness comes only from our increasing sense of perfection which we can achieve only through self-transcendence. But right now the world has not come up to that standard.

A Great Champion

A great champion is he who wins all the races.

A great champion is he who participates in all the races.

A great champion is he who does not care for the results of the races – whether he is first or last or in between. He races just to get joy and give joy to the observers.

A great champion is he who transcends his own previous records.

A great champion is he who maintains his standard.

A great champion is he who remains happy even when he cannot maintain his standard.

A great champion is he who has established his inseparable oneness with the winner and the loser alike.

A great champion is he who, owing to the advancement of years, retires from racing or terminates his career happily and cheerfully.

A great champion is he who longs to see the fulfilment of his dreams – if not through himself, then in and through others. It does not even have to be in and through his own dear ones; it can be in and through any human being on earth. If someone who could not manifest his own dreams is extremely happy when he sees his vision being manifested into reality through somebody else, then he is a really great champion.

A great champion is he who meditates on his Inner Pilot for the fulfilment of His Will before the race, during the race and after the race.

A great champion is he who sees and feels that he is a mere instrument of his Inner Pilot and that his Inner Pilot is racing in and through him, according to his own capacity of receptivity.

A champion of champions is he whose inner life has become the Vision of his Absolute Supreme and whose outer life has become the perfection-channel of his Beloved Supreme.

Yesterday
I measured my success
By competing with others.

Today
I measure my success
By competing with myself.

Tomorrow
I shall measure my success
By expanding my heart
To encompass others.

There is no ultimate limit
To an athlete's performance.

CHAPTER TEN

Beyond the Age Barrier

 *The soul teaches the body*
Never to accept
Any limitation.

Age is in the Mind, Not in the Heart

Sri Chinmoy made the following remarks in Sacramento, California, on 1 June 1996 after competing in the California State Senior Games:

The younger you can become, the faster will be your progress. This is absolutely no joke! I am fast approaching sixty-five years of age. I shall do a few more things in this lifetime which I could not do in my adolescent years. I have already done the head balance, which I could never do, even when I was a champion athlete. And there are five or six more things I shall do in this incarnation which, at the time of my athletic career, I could not do. If you sincerely want to make faster progress, you have to have a childlike heart. It is the mind that makes us feel we are too old, we are useless. This mind has to be silenced by the will of the heart, by the will of the soul.

It is the light of the soul that can illumine the mind. True, it is a very, very long process, but the mind can be illumined eventually. If you silence the mind, the mind becomes like a tame and faithful dog.

Age is in the mind; age is not in the body. When we think that we are old, that is the end, the very end, of our journey. Every day at every moment only think that you are a seven-year-old or a nine-year-old or a ten-year-old, but do not think that you are over thirty. Do not make it into thirty-one and absolutely not into forty-one! If you cannot make yourself into a seven-year-old child, then at the maximum think of thirteen. Just imagine! Imagination is a reality of its own. Imagination is a world of its own, but you have to bring down that world every day or you have to enter into that world.

Even if you do not want to take exercise early in the morning, try to make yourself feel that you are quite young. Just go outside and see what happens. Then, while you are walking, try to walk a little faster. While you are doing anything, make the movement faster. Bring back your childlike days when you used to run and play with utmost joy. At the age of thirteen or fourteen I ran. It is quite natural for a teenager to run. But at the age of sixty-five if I run, it means I am trying to maintain some joy, some enthusiasm.

With determination we can conquer the age barrier and go back to our childlike heart, where hope is blossoming at every moment. If we can remain in the heart, then we can act like a child and there will be no end to our progress. Our old-age bondage-limitations will be transformed once more into our childhood-freedom-dreams.

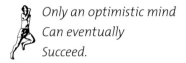

Only an optimistic mind
Can eventually
Succeed.

Carl Lewis *on preparing for his fourth Olympics (1996) at age 35:*

When I became 30 or 35 years old, I heard always how old I was. Even though every single day I would hear 'You are too old, you can't do it,' I really stayed focused on what I could do. And when I won a second gold in the hundred metres in 1988, I was the oldest gold medallist and the only one to repeat that win. When I set the world record in the 100 metres in 1991, I was the oldest world-record holder. And in the long jump in Atlanta I was the oldest long jump champion.

"Sri Chinmoy told me about this: 'You have to forget about your age. Be thirteen. Always think of this number, thirteen, and keep the energy and desire of someone who is thirteen. Then you will always be young. You will always run young.'"

Sri Chinmoy made these comments at the V World Masters Games, held in San Juan, Puerto Rico, in September 1983 where he participated in several events:

In order to make progress we have to be with the world, in the world and for the world. We like peace, love and the feeling of oneness. Because of our feeling of oneness, because of our love of peace, we have come to the World Masters Games. People from various countries have come to these Games to show their feeling of oneness.

These Masters Games offer us a special message. They make us feel that even though we may be forty, fifty, sixty, seventy, eighty or even ninety years old, we are still God's children. When someone is fifty years old, it is very difficult for him to think of himself as a child. For us to think of ourselves as children is very difficult because we have developed the mind. But the Masters Games help us feel that we are truly children, for it is only children who like to play. People who are advanced in years will stay home and watch television or read newspapers, but children have boundless energy. They have hope, they have ambition, they have determination. They want to become good, better, best.

Most of the time, elderly people feel that they are finished products, that their life is over. So they do not have any hope or promise. But the Masters Games show us that elderly people can have hope and promise. It shows that elderly people can become inseparably one with children, with the new generation.

There is no age limit. When we pray and meditate, we go far beyond the domain of the mind, the physical mind that doubts our capacities.

These masters athletes are challenging their own self-doubt. They are shaking hands smilingly and proudly with impossibility. People say, "It is impossible – a person of that age cannot do pole vault. They cannot do shot put or hurdles." But these masters athletes are proving that there is no such thing as impossibility.

The Spirit of the Masters Games

There is every possibility that the World Masters Games will become very popular in terms of bringing real joy to mankind. In the Olympics, each individual is trying to get a gold medal. But the real meaning behind the gold medal is joy. A grandfather may not bring back a gold medal but he brings back joy. He comes all the way from an obscure village to compete, and when he goes back home, his grandchildren are not going to ask him, "Can you show me your gold medal?" No, the fact that he has gotten such joy from competing is enough. This grandfather perhaps for many months did not smile, thinking of his sport or collecting money to come to Puerto Rico. But now the whole family is seeing that the grandfather is so happy. If the father sees that the son has become an Olympian, he will be so proud. Similarly, if the son sees that the father has gotten real joy by participating in these Masters Games, it will be a happy family. One individual has come from an Indian village and another has come from an Australian village. When they go back to their countries and speak to their children, grandchildren, friends and neighbours about the Games, and when others see such joy in them, then this joy will spread like wildfire in their village, town, city and country.

Most of the athletes are not expecting to break any record; they are happy just to participate and get innocent joy. But many Olympic athletes will go home really miserable because they had come for a gold medal and perhaps did not even get the bronze. But in the Masters Games, even if your place is last, you are very happy.

It is like the difference between amateurs and professionals. In tennis, for example, as soon as people become good players, they turn professional so that they can become millionaires overnight. Then the real joy goes away from the game. In the Olympics, the athletes are not getting money; they are just getting gold medals. But still, much of the joy has disappeared from the competition. So many people are looking for name and fame for their countries, and the prestige of all the countries is at stake. The countries spend thousands and thousands of dollars on the athletes, and there are so many businesses that act as sponsors. But in the Masters Games, everybody came at their own expense just for the joy of competing. If they can continue like this – doing everything at their own expense – then they will continue getting pure joy and giving pure joy to mankind.

The world is crying for joy, and I think the Masters Games will give more joy because the competition is not on such a vital plane. Here, in the competition there is a psychic touch. People have become more mature over the years; they have gone through success and failure many, many times. When they were young, almost all of them had the same kind of qualities that the young ones have today. But now that they are older, they do not want to manifest these qualities. They are looking only to give and receive joy. Here you have people from various countries coming together and making friends. If I come here and make a friend, and if we both become friends with someone else, then how can there ever be any conflicts in the world? These types of games give us a golden opportunity to become one family, and they contribute tremendously to the joy of the world-family.

CHAPTER ELEVEN

World Peace Through Meditation and Sport

*If you can create harmony
In your own life,
This harmony will enter
Into the vast world.*

Creating World Peace

I feel that while running we are able to offer our very best to establish a world of peace.

There shall come a time when this world of ours will be flooded with peace. Who is going to bring about this radical change? It will be you, you and your brothers and sisters. You and your oneness-heart will spread peace throughout the length and breadth of the world.

***Tegla Loroupe** of Kenya with the winners of the 2011 Tegla Loroupe Peace Race, who used to make a living using illegal arms. Tegla uses her success in running to encourage young people to give up guns and endorse alternative sources of livelihood.*

In a positive way, this world of ours will be liberated from misunderstanding, quarrels, fights, wars and all kinds of limitation and weakness. It will be a happy and illumining oneness-family. It is only a matter of time before each individual will start praying and meditating consciously and become a choice instrument of God. Then the oneness-home that this world truly is, will not remain and cannot remain a far cry.

 Yesterday I was clever.
That is why
I wanted to change the world.

Today I am wise.
That is why
I am changing myself.

When I feel inner strength, at that time I have peace of mind and I do not want to quarrel or fight. We quarrel and fight precisely because inwardly we feel that we are weak. For a human being, the only way to become really strong is to pray and meditate. When we pray and meditate, we develop inner strength, and this inner strength is nothing other than peace.

If everybody brings to the fore his own inner strength, the world will eventually be inundated with peace. Peace is oneness, oneness is peace. If I am strong and you are strong, then definitely we have established our oneness, and this oneness is nothing other than peace.

It is individuals who are responsible not only for their own lives but also for their countries and also for the entire world. It is from individuals that the message-light of inner strength can and will enter into nations. And, when oneness-light-strength enters into the nations, there will be no more war. It will all be oneness-song.

The inner life and the outer life must go together. If I pray early in the morning, then I will have good thoughts towards others, I will have love for them. If everyone does the same, then there will be no quarrel, no fight. Everything has to come from within. From within, it comes without. If we have peace of mind, a moment of joy deep inside us, then this joy we express outwardly. Whatever we have within, we manifest in our outer life. If we have anxiety, worry, insecurity and other undivine qualities, then this is what we will manifest outwardly. But if we pray and meditate early in the morning, inwardly we become good citizens of the world. Then in our outer activities we will try to express our inner good feelings. This is how we can establish a oneness-family.

World peace
Can be achieved
When the power of love
Replaces
The love of power.

I believe that harmony within oneself and with the rest of the world is a key factor for athletic success and a happy balanced life. It can make a difference between winning and losing, in life or within your chosen sport. It is a fact that sport brings people together, like music does for instance. The more people getting involved in a peaceful sport, the better the world will be!"

—François Gay

" Sport has incredible potential to promote peace and harmony in the world. Sport is a language that everyone can speak. It is not about the colour of your skin, your religion, your wealth, your disability – it is about being the best you can be. It is a wonderful foundation for life and for creating harmony in the world."

—**Katrina Webb**, Australian Paralympics Champion

" To make sport is for me like seeing the world as a family. I come from a conflict region. Although I was training and racing mostly in Europe, at the end of the day there was a feeling in my heart that I should do something to help those at home suffering from conflicts. That's how I developed the idea to use sport to promote peace to bring people together.

"I was not sure about how to do it. When I met Sri Chinmoy in 1999 at the United Nations in New York, he presented to me the Abebe Bikila Award of the New York Road Runners Club. He told me on that occasion, 'Tegla, when you run, think of others and preach peace.'

"So I started organising Peace Races in Africa in 2003. The annual Tegla Loroupe Peace Race is a perfect example of how sports can be used for positive gains within the community. The 2010 edition managed to bring together over 200 warriors from warring pastoralist communities drawn from Kenya, Uganda and Southern Sudan.

"I feel we as athletes have to be role models to other people and this also means in respect to working for peace and harmony in the world."

—**Tegla Loroupe**, Kenyan former Marathon World Record Holder
and global spokeswoman for peace

 ↑

Katrina Webb from Australia won gold medals in the 100 m and 200 m and a silver medal in the long jump at her first Paralympic Games in Atlanta in 1996. In 2005, Katrina supported the United Nations Year of Sport for Development and Peace, highlighting the importance of sport for improving the lives of people with disabilities.

↗

The Tegla Loroupe Peace Races have been held since 2003 to promote peaceful co-existence among pastoral communities in Kenya and Uganda. "I can contribute something to the world: Peace through Sport" is the motto.

The Sri Chinmoy Oneness-Home Peace Run

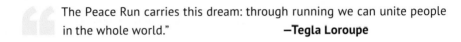

> The Peace Run carries this dream: through running we can unite people in the whole world."   **—Tegla Loroupe**

The Peace Run, also known as the World Harmony Run, was founded by Sri Chinmoy in 1987. Every two years epic events are organised in Europe, Africa, North America, Asia and Australasia in which teams of relay runners carry a flaming Peace Torch. As they pass the torch from hand to hand and from heart to heart, they also carry the hope of peace and harmony between nations.

Along the route, people of all nationalities, faiths and traditions are invited to participate in this event. From children to seniors, from everyday citizens to world leaders, people join the runners by carrying the torch for a few steps or a few miles. In visits to schools along the route, the message of global friendship and goodwill is shared with schoolchildren and teachers who add their own wishes for a peaceful and harmonious world.

> When I carried the flaming torch, I felt so much oneness with all the people of the world. Each participant in the Peace Run will show that the hopes and dreams of man are more enduring than his fears. And the trials on the road to world-peace are no greater than the courage of those who accept the challenge."
>
> **—Carl Lewis**

Peace begins with me. *The motto of the Peace Run becoming the reality.*

Tatyana Lebedeva holding the Peace Torch together with her daughter.

↗
From sea to shining sea. Members of the US Peace Run team make
their way through all 50 states in the Union.

Today's chaotic world cannot forever remain chaotic. World harmony, world peace: these are not mere dictionary words. These are realities, divine realities and supreme realities. For all of us who are aspiring to become good citizens of the world, our Peace Run is a supremely important inspiration to all of us.

True, our physical bodies have not been and will not be able to cover the length and breath of the world. But the spirit that we have deep within, and the spirit that we truly are, has covered the length and breath of the world many, many times.

—**Sri Chinmoy**

Transcendence is perfection.
Perfection is transcendence.
When we transcend our capacities,
Immediately we get an inner joy,
An inner thrill,
Which is another name for perfection.
No perfection can ever be achieved
Without self-transcendence.

APPENDIX A

The Sri Chinmoy Marathon Team

Sri Chinmoy founded the Sri Chinmoy Marathon Team in 1977 as a service to the running community and to help promote spiritual growth through sports.

Over the years, the Sri Chinmoy Marathon Team has become one of the world's largest organisers of ultra-distance running and a major organiser of road races, marathons, triathlons, multi-sport events, long-distance swimming events and Master's track-and-field meets. It has hosted several national championships, and numerous world records have been set in its races.

In the early years of the 'running boom', these events established standards and levels of service to participants that have now become commonplace in ultra-races: regular drink stations, post-race food and prizes through all the age groups up to 70+ years.

Sri Chinmoy's belief in our own limitless potential led him to create endurance events that seemed beyond the realms of human possibility – the prime example being the 3100-Mile Self-Transcendence Race, first held in 1997, which remains the longest certified road race in the world.

Many Sri Chinmoy Marathon Team members have performed remarkable feats in different disciplines over the years, showing that, indeed, anything is possible if one simply has faith in oneself. Perhaps the most well-known of them is Ashrita Furman *(www.ashrita.com)*. Ashrita has set over 350 Guinness world records in many disciplines, including the fastest five mile run on stilts and pogo stick jumping up Mt. Fuji, Japan (16 miles).

Many of the Team's members have swum the English Channel, and several of them hold or have held distance records for running in various countries. Team members in over 60 countries also participate in cycling, triathlon, track and field and mountaineering events.

Contact & Links

Sri Chinmoy Marathon Team
International Headquarters
150-47 87th Ave.
Jamaica, NY 11432, USA

www.**srichinmoyraces**.org *(including local contact information)*
www.**peacerun**.org
www.**srichinmoybooks**.com *(including titles in other languages)*
www.**inspiration-lifts**.org *(featuring videos of some of Sri Chinmoy's lifts)*
www.**srichinmoy**.org

Explanatory Notes

Yoga

Yoga is the discipline of the body, mind and spirit, having its roots in ancient India. In the western hemisphere, Yoga is most often known as the practice of specific body postures as in Hatha Yoga. In the eastern hemisphere and as referred to in this book, yoga is understood as the practice of leading a spiritual life. The practice of yoga focuses on self knowledge and self-discovery. This may include prayer or meditation, one's work life, physical exercise and service to humanity.

Through the sustained practice of yoga we are able to consciously experience our oneness with others and eventually, with all of existence. The meaning of yoga in Sanskrit is union. In Sri Chinmoy's words: "It is the union of the individual soul with the Supreme Self. Yoga is the spiritual science that teaches us how the Ultimate Reality can be realised in life itself."

There are many paths of yoga but ultimately we must each find our own way to Truth. Sri Chinmoy writes: "Freedom, absolute freedom, must be given each individual soul to discover its own path."

The Vital

According to Indian spiritual philosophy the vital is the part of our being, which houses ordinary desires and demands as well as the human emotions connected with them. Depending on the evolution and the nature of a human being, the vital is more or less domineering and aggressive. Sri Chinmoy explains: "For an ordinary person, the aggressive vital is normal and necessary. But for a spiritual person, the vital does not always have to be aggressive. It can become pure and dynamic. The vital is located in the navel area."

Aspiration

Aspiration is the inner mounting cry of our soul for perfection and truth. It is the conscious cry to climb up to the highest ultimate Goal. This inner cry we can feel inside our spiritual heart.

The Spiritual Heart

The spiritual heart is an energy centre (Anahata chakra) located in the centre of the chest, in the centre of our existence, where it is felt that our soul resides. The spiritual heart is approximately twelve finger-breadths directly above the navel.

Supreme

"There is one God called by many different names. I like the term 'Supreme'. All religious faiths worship the same God, but they address Him differently. A man will be called 'Father' by one person, 'Brother' by another and 'Uncle' by another. Similarly, God is also addressed in various ways, according to one's sweetest, most affectionate feeling. I get a sweeter feeling from using the term 'Supreme' instead of saying 'God' or 'Father'.

"When we say 'Supreme', we are speaking of the Supreme Lord who not only reaches the absolute Highest, but all the time goes beyond, beyond and transcends the Beyond."

(Excerpted from Sri Chinmoy's writings)

Supreme Pilot and Inner Pilot

Our inner guide, our own highest Self who guides us. Sri Chinmoy used the term 'Inner Pilot' for the Supreme within us who guides us.

Purity

"Doubt, insincerity, fear, anxiety, jealousy, attachment and all other imperfections or limitations are impurities. Impurity includes insincerity, doubt and all other negative ways of thinking and it is bound to affect both our outer behaviour and our inner progress.

"Whenever you feel aggression, it is impurity; and when you feel divine dynamism, it is purity.

"Purity is the light of our soul expressing its divinity through the body, the vital and the mind. Purity is the Breath of the Supreme. Purity means following the dictates of our Inner Pilot without allowing undivine forces to enter into us."

(Excerpted from Sri Chinmoy's writings)

Seeker

"What has been lost? Our conscious oneness with the Absolute Supreme has been lost. Through our inner search we are trying to gain or regain our conscious inseparable oneness with him. We are seeking for Truth and Light. Once upon a time, we were possessors of this infinite Truth and Light. But unfortunately, we made friends with ignorance-night and lost our inseparable oneness with Infinity's Light and Bliss. It is through conscious seeking – our conscious inner search and inner mounting cry – that at God's choice Hour we shall once again get back our inner wealth."

(Excerpted from Sri Chinmoy's writings)

The Third Eye

The third eye is the eye of inner vision, the vision that goes beyond what the physical eyes can see; the vision that can see into the past and into the future. The third eye is the energy centre called the Ajna chakra located on the forehead between and slightly above the eyebrows.

Subtle Channels

"Prana is the life-energy or life-principle of the universe. There are three principal channels through which this life-energy flows. These channels are *Ida*, *Pingala* and *Sushumna*. In Sanskrit these channels are called *nadis*. Ida, pingala and sushumna are inside our subtle physical body, not inside the gross physical. Ida carries the current of life-energy in the left side of the body. Pingala carries the current in the right side of the body. Sushumna carries the current in the middle of the spinal column. Sushumna is the most important of the three nadis. It receives a ceaseless stream of life-energy from the universal Consciousness-light."

(Excerpted from Sri Chinmoy's writings)

Sources (in alphabetical order)

A Galaxy of Beauty's Stars, *Agni Press, 1974*

A Mystic Journey in the Weightlifting World, *Part 1, Agni Press, 2000*

A Seeker Is a Singer, *Agni Press, 1987*

Arise! Awake! Thoughts of a Yogi, *New York Frederick Fell, Inc., 1972*

Aspiration-Body, Illumination-Soul, *Parts 1–3, Agni Press, 1987*

Aspiration-Body, Illumination-Soul, *Part 3, Agni Press, 2004*

Aspiration-Body, Illumination-Soul, *Part 4, Agni Press, 1987*

Body, Heart & Soul One-Arm Lift Anniversary 25-26 June 1986, *Agni Press, 1986*

Canada Aspires, Canada Receives, Canada Achieves, *Part 1, Agni Press, 1974*

Carl Lewis: The Champion Inner Runner, *Agni Press, 1991*

Chandelier, *Part 2, Agni Press, 1981*

Conversations with Sri Chinmoy, *Agni Press, 2007*

Creation and Perfection, *Agni Press, 1976*

Earth's Cry Meets Heaven's Smile, *Book 3, Aum Press, 1978*

Eastern Light for the Western Mind, *Aum Publications, 1989*

Eternity's Breath, *Sri Chinmoy Lighthouse, 1975*

Fifty Freedom-Boats to One Golden Shore, *Parts 1, 2, 3, Agni Press, 1974*

Flame Waves, *Part 4, Agni Press, 1975*

Flame Waves, *Part 12, Agni Press, 1978*

Flame-Goal, *Agni Press, 1973*

Four Hundred Gratitude-Flower-Hearts, *Agni Press, 1979*

God the Supreme Musician, *Sri Chinmoy Lighthouse, 1974*

I Am My Life's God-Hunger-Heart, *Part 4, Agni Press, 1994*

I Pray Before I Lift, I Meditate While I Lift, I Offer My Gratitude-Cries and Gratitude-Smiles, *Agni Press, 1986*

Inner Progress and Satisfaction-Life, *Agni Press, 1977*

Kundalini: The Mother-Power, *Agni Press, 1974*

Lifting Up the World with a Oneness-Heart, *Agni Press, 1988*

Man is Man's Eternal Race Because God is God's Infinite Grace, *Agni Press, 1990*

Meditation: Man-Perfection in God-Satisfaction, *AUM Publications, 1989*

Meditation: God's Duty and Man's Beauty, *Agni Press, 1974*

Meditation: Humanity's Race and Divinity's Grace, *Part 2, Agni Press, 1974*

Meditation: Man's Choice and God's Voice *Part 1, 2, Agni Press, 1974*

My Christmas-New Year-Vacation-Aspiration-Prayers, *Part 52, 57, Agni Press 2007–2008*

My Fifty Gratitude-Summers, *Agni Press, 1981*

My Heart's Salutation to Australia, *Part 2, Agni Press, 1976*

My Meditation-Service at the United Nations for 25 Years, *Agni Press, 1995*

My Morning Soul-Body Prayers, *Part 8, Agni Press, 1999*

My Rose Petals, *Part 1, Sri Chinmoy Centre Inc, 1971*

My Rose Petals, *Part 4, Sri Chinmoy Lighthouse, 1974*

My Rose Petals, *Part 7, Agni Press, 1976*

My Weightlifting Tears and Smiles, *Part 2, Agni Press, 1986*

No Unreachable Goal, *Agni Press, 1994*

Peace-Blossoms on the Philippine Life-Tree, *Agni Press, 1993*

Peace-Lovers, *Professors for Peace, 1997*

Perfection-World, *Agni Press, 1974*

Perseverance and Aspiration, *Aum Publications, 1976*

Pioneer-Runners of Tomorrow's World-Peace-Dawn, *Agni Press, 1998*

Problems! Problems! Are They Really Problems? Part 2,
    Sri Chinmoy Lighthouse, 1974

Purity: Divinity's Little Sister, *Agni Press, 1974*

Purity-River Wins, *Agni Press, 1974*

Rainbow-Dreams, *Agni Press, 1996*

Rainbow-Flowers, *Part 1, 1973*

Run and Become, Become And Run, *Songbook, Agni Press, 1982*

Run and Smile, Smile and Run, *Agni Press, 2000*

Runner's Gazette column, *May 1982 and January 1987*

Seventy-Seven Thousand Service-Trees, *Parts 1, 5, 11, 13, 14, 15, 16, 19, 47, 48, Agni Press, 1998–2007*

Sleep: Death's Little Sister, *Agni Press, 1974*

Soul-Illumination-Shrine, Body-Preparation-Temple, *Part 1, Agni Press, 1985*

Sri Chinmoy Answers, *Parts 2, 12, 16, 24, 26, 28, 29, 33, 34, 35, Agni Press, 1995–2004*

Sri Chinmoy Speaks, *Part 1, 4, Agni Press, 1976*

Talk about Running the New York Marathon (unpublished), *New York, 29 Oct 1986*

Ten Thousand Flower-Flames, *Parts 4, 16, 17, 18, 28, 39, 44, 76, 93, 96, 98, Agni Press, 1979–1983*

The Body: Humanity's Fortress, *Agni Press, 1974*

The Dance of Life, *Part 2, 19*

The Divine Hero, *Watkins Publishing London, 2002*

The God of the Mind, *Agni Press, 1989*

The Hunger of Darkness and the Feast of Light, *Part 2, Agni Press, 1974*

The Inner Meaning of Sport, *Agni Press, 2007*

The Inner Running and the Outer Running, *Aum Publications, 2008*

The Inner World and the Outer World, *Agni Press, 1988*

The Life-Illumining Traveller's Companion, *Series 1, Agni Press, 1993*

The Luminous Life of Sri Chinmoy, *Tiny Tot Publications Delhi, India, 2005*

The Master and the Disciple, *Agni Press, 1985*

The New Day Beckons. A Traveller's Companion, *Series 2, Agni Press, 1994*

The Outer Running and the Inner Running, *Agni Press, 1984*

The Silent Teaching, *Agni Press, 1984*

The Spiritual Life, *Agni Press, 1984*

The Sri Chinmoy Runner's Logbook, *1981*

The Vision of God's Dawn, *Agni Press, 1974*

The Vision-Sky of California, *Agni Press, 1980*

The Wings of Joy, *Simon & Schuster, New York, 1997*

Twenty-Seven Thousand Aspiration-Plants, *Parts 3, 14, 16, 19, 95, 109, 131, 133, 188, 216, 224, 237, 239, Agni Press, 1983–1997*

United Nations Meditation-Flowers and Tomorrow's Noon, *Agni Press, 1978*

World Harmony Run Talk (unpublished), *New York, 6 July 2005*

Yes, I Can! I Certainly Can!!, *Agni Press, 2000*

Yoga and the Spiritual Life, *Aum Publications, 1996*

We would like to thank all the photographers whose photos
have appeared in this book.

Photo credits *(page number)*:

Alphafoto *(151)*
Dreamstime *(front cover, 25)*
François Gay's archive *(129)*
iStockphoto *(front cover, 47, 126, 136)*
Katrina Webb's archive *(181)*
Olivier Bernhard's archive *(1)*
Reuters *(118)*
Robert Boesch *(29, 30)*
Shutterstock *(51)*
Sri Chinmoy Centre photographers *(front & back cover, 17, 22, 43, 49, 60, 63, 65, 66,
    67, 69, 70, 72, 76, 77, 80, 83, 84, 89, 91, 92, 95, 105, 106, 112, 117, 122, 128, 147,
    155, 157, 161, 176, 181, 183, 184, 185)*
Tatyana Lebedeva's archive *(184)*